# New York

# New York

*Ann Heinrichs*

Children's Press®
A Division of Grolier Publishing
New York   London   Hong Kong   Sydney
Danbury, Connecticut

**Frontispiece: The Statue of Liberty**

**Front cover: The Empire State Building**

**Back cover: Niagara Falls**

Consultant: Elaine Clark, Senior Librarian, New York State Library

*Please note: All statistics are as up-to-date as possible at the time of publication.*

Visit Children's Press on the Internet at http://publishing.grolier.com

Book production by Editorial Directions, Inc.

Library of Congress Cataloging-in-Publication Data

Heinrichs, Ann.
    New York / by Ann Heinrichs.
        144 p. 24 cm. — (America the beautiful. Second series)
    Includes bibliographical references and index.
    Summary : Describes the geography, plants, animals, history, economy, language, religions, culture, sports, art, and people of the state of New York.
    ISBN 0-516-20691-5
    1. New York (State)—Juvenile literature. [1. New York (State)] I.Heinrichs, Ann. II. New York. II. Title. III. Series.
    F119.3.H45    1999
    974.7—dc21                                                        98-27784
                                                                            CIP
                                                                            A

## Acknowledgments

For their kind assistance in this project, I am grateful to innumerable employees of New York's state library and archives, department of economic development, and travel and tourism association; and to all the New Yorkers who shared their visions and experiences with me.

Niagara Falls

The Empire State Building

Binghamton

# Contents

A Thomas Nast drawing

**West Point Academy**

**Ellis Island**

**Skiing in the Adirondacks**

**The Chrysler Building**

# "I Love New York"

**J**oel plays soccer, studies violin, and belongs to the drama and math clubs. On his weekend wanderings, he winds past the savory smells of Chinese, Indian, and Lebanese restaurants. Eventually, he reaches his favorite lookout point, the Promenade— at the end of Montague Street in Brooklyn Heights, on a high ridge overlooking the East River.

From there, he gazes out toward the Statue of Liberty and thinks of his great-grandfather. The old man was not much older than Joel when he saw most of his family killed in Russia. How thrilled he must have been, after months of grueling travel, to peer out from belowdecks at the glistening statue.

In the other direction is a magnificent view of Manhattan skyscrapers. From Joel's tree-lined neighborhood in Brooklyn, it's only a twenty-minute subway ride to the vibrant heart of Manhattan. There he can hear his violin teacher play with the New York Philharmonic in Lincoln Center. His drama class takes field trips into Manhattan, too. They take in the latest Broadway musicals, as well as exciting new off-Broadway plays.

When summer rolls around, it's time for camp. Like thousands of New York "city kids," Joel packs up his gear and loads it into the family car. His parents drive north—far beyond the traffic and the noise. The city skyline disappears into the haze, and before long, they're in the cool, wooded mountains of upstate New York.

**Fall comes early in the hills of Binghamton, along Interstate 88.**

**Opposite: An aerial view of lower Manhattan and the harbor**

After six weeks of rock climbing, wilderness hiking, river rafting, archery, and soccer, Joel is ready to chill. His parents pick him up, and they head for the family's farm. No signs point the way, but Joel knows the route by heart. Left at the pond, right at the old mill, take the curve past the crumbling stone wall.

It's pretty wild in this part of central New York State. Joel's parents have cleared only half an acre so far, but it's here Joel relaxes, explores, and dreams. At night, when he hears the coyotes howl under the starry sky, New York City might as well be a thousand miles away.

By August, he's getting restless. Truly a child of the city, Joel loves commotion and a good challenge. His heart pumps faster just thinking of the coming year's tryouts, tournaments, shows, and exams.

Like many residents, Joel is at home in both of New York's "two worlds." One world is New York City—a "concrete jungle" of towering skyscrapers above a sea of yellow taxis. Nicknamed the Big Apple, it's big in every way. It's the financial and cultural capital of the world, where hard work, competition, and speed are the ways to succeed. Just try crossing a downtown street, and you'll see why "in a New York minute" means "fast," and "in a New York second" means *"incredibly* fast."

The other world is upstate New York—almost all the rest of the state. Upstate is a rolling panorama of villages and small towns, of apple orchards, vineyards, and dairy farms. For weary city-dwellers, upstate offers a great escape—a chance to enjoy the cool mountain air of the Adirondacks and the Catskills and the clear waters of the Finger Lakes.

Not many residents can sing the state song of New York. But they repeat its title time and again. No matter which of the two worlds they come from, New Yorkers are quick to declare loudly: "I Love New York!"

# CHAPTER TWO

# Out of the Wilderness

**An early lithograph depicting a Manhattan village prior to Dutch settlement**

ome streets in Brooklyn today are the same routes the Indians took between villages. Before Europeans arrived, the Canarsee Indians had settlements in Brooklyn and Staten Island. They were among the hundreds of Algonquin-speaking Indian groups that lived across North America.

More than a dozen Algonquin groups lived in present-day New York. Manhattan Indians occupied the northern part of today's Manhattan Island, and the Rockaways lived in Queens. Other Algonquins were the Montauk, Munsee, Delaware, Wappinger, and Mahican, or Mohican. They lived along the coast and in the Hudson River Valley.

Algonquins raised maize (corn), beans, and squash. Their homes were long wooden structures called longhouses which held fifty people or more. With the cooking fires burning, the longhouses were smoky inside.

The Iroquois occupied the inland forests, covering most of present-day New York State. Their member nations included the Cayuga, Mohawk, Oneida, Onondaga, and Seneca. In the eighteenth century, the Tuscarora from North Carolina joined them. The Iroquois, too, built wooden longhouses. Some were as long as 200 feet (61 m).

**Opposite: Autumn in the Adirondacks**

Iroquois women farmed, cooked, and tended to household chores. In the winter, the men hunted and trapped animals in the forest. Summertime was the time for making war. Iroquois attacks cut down much of New York's Algonquin population. But various Iroquois tribes brutalized one another, too. One tribe's killing called for another tribe's revenge.

After years of bloody warfare with one another, the Iroquois met in a great peace council. According to legend, a warrior named Ayawentha, or Hiawatha, brought the meeting together. Bitter over the murder of his family, he had withdrawn to the forest. Then one night, he dreamed of a god who told him to lead the Iroquois nation to peace. The Iroquois joined together to form the powerful Iroquois Confederacy in about 1570. Into this setting, European explorers arrived.

The discovery of the Hudson River

## Explorers

Giovanni da Verrazano was the first European to reach New York. He was an Italian navigator hired by the king of France to explore North America. In 1524, he sailed into present-day New York Harbor.

The Englishman Henry Hudson was the next to arrive. He sailed a ship for the Dutch East India Company, merchant explorers of the Netherlands. Hudson's mission was to find the Northwest Passage—a water route

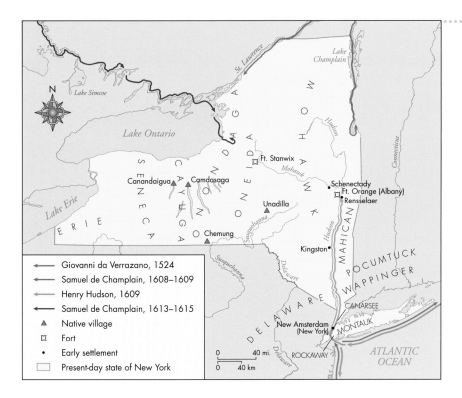

Exploration map of
New York

across North America to the Pacific Ocean. That would give the Dutch company a way to get to Asia's spices, silks, and precious jewels.

On his ship the *Half Moon*, Hudson and his handful of sailors reached the mouth of the Hudson River in 1609. He sailed up the river as far as Albany, writing detailed descriptions as he went along. The Dutch were disappointed in Hudson's discoveries. But because of his voyage, the Netherlands was able to claim much of New York and other lands along the North Atlantic.

In the same year, 1609, the Frenchman Samuel de Champlain was exploring New York from another direction. He entered northeastern New York from the Canadian province of Quebec. That gave France a claim to New York, too.

Peter Minuit purchasing Manhattan Island from the Indians

## New Netherland

The Netherlands named its North American territory New Netherland. Dutch traders set up forts and trading posts along the Hudson and traded with the Indians for furs. Dutch merchants soon learned that there was money to be made in the fur trade. Beaver and otter pelts made luxurious hats and coats for European markets. A group of traders formed the Dutch West India Company, and their government gave them trading rights in all of New Netherland.

Now the Dutch were ready to settle in for the long term. The company gathered up thirty families—about 110 men, women, and children—and sailed to New Netherland. Most of the settlers were French Protestants called Huguenots, who were fleeing religious persecution in France. In 1624, they established Fort Orange, now the city of Albany. It was the colony's first permanent white settlement.

Another group of colonists settled on the southern end of Manhattan Island. In 1625, they built a town and named it New Amsterdam. As new families arrived, the town grew. One official wrote back to the Netherlands that the people of New Amsterdam "are of good cheer and live peaceably." The letter included another bit of news about a land deal.

Peter Minuit, the Dutch governor-general, wanted to make the New Amsterdam settlement legal. He made a bargain with local Indians to buy the entire island of Manhattan. In payment, Minuit gave them trade goods worth sixty Dutch guilders. At the time, that was equal to about twenty-four dollars.

## The Colony Expands

Meanwhile, other settlers built towns in present-day Brooklyn, Kingston, Rensselaer, and Schenectady. To help fill up the colony, the Dutch West India Company granted enormous tracts of land to its members. If they could bring in fifty settlers within four years, they could keep the land.

These landowners, called patroons, rented plots of farmland to tenant farmers. Kiliaen Van Rensselaer was the first to receive a patroonship. His estate stretched for 20 miles (32 km) along the Hudson River near Albany. For poor immigrants or newcomers from other colonies, tenant farming was a welcome choice. At the

**New Amsterdam**

same time, it discouraged pioneers who wanted land of their own.

Peter Stuyvesant became governor of the colony in 1647. He arrived in New Amsterdam with a wooden leg and a bad temper and tried to put the town in order. Under Stuyvesant, the streets were paved with cobblestones and a city council was put in place. Neat, Dutch-style houses lined the avenues. At the north end of the settlement stood a barrier of posts to protect against Indian raids. It was called *de wal*—Dutch for the wall. Today, Manhattan's Wall Street runs along that same boundary line.

## A Haven for All

Unlike many of the other American colonies, New Netherland tolerated all religions. Quakers and other religious groups moved in from other colonies. Jewish people were another early immigrant group. They began settling in New Amsterdam in the 1650s.

All nationalities were welcomed, too. By the 1660s, more than 1,500 people lived in New Amsterdam, and more than fifteen languages were spoken there. Along the Hudson River were farmers from France, Denmark, Norway, Sweden, England, Germany, Poland, Portugal, and Italy.

New Netherlanders also enjoyed a more relaxed and open social life than other colonists. There were boisterous inns for drinking and dancing. Holidays such as Christmas and New Year's

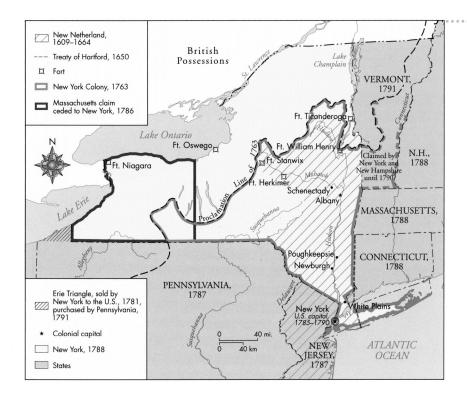

**Territorial map of New York**

*Legend:*
- New Netherland, 1609–1664
- Treaty of Hartford, 1650
- Fort
- New York Colony, 1763
- Massachusetts claim ceded to New York, 1786
- Erie Triangle, sold by New York to the U.S., 1781, purchased by Pennsylvania, 1791
- ★ Colonial capital
- New York, 1788
- States

*Map labels:*
British Possessions
VERMONT, 1791
Ft. Ticonderoga
Lake Champlain
Lake Ontario
Ft. Oswego
Ft. Niagara
Lake Erie
Ft. William Henry
Ft. Stanwix
Ft. Herkimer
Schenectady
Albany
N.H., 1788
Claimed by New York and New Hampshire until 1790
MASSACHUSETTS, 1788
CONNECTICUT, 1788
Poughkeepsie
Newburgh
PENNSYLVANIA, 1787
White Plains
New York U.S. capital, 1785–1790
NEW JERSEY, 1787
ATLANTIC OCEAN
N

were times for feasting and merrymaking. Popular sports included boat and carriage races and the Dutch game of *kolf*, the ancestor of golf.

## The British

New Netherland was a nuisance to England. Along the Atlantic coast—both north and south of New Netherland—were British colonies. England controlled all the shipping through the colonies' ports. But traders could get around England's strict shipping laws by sailing in and out of New Amsterdam. King Charles of England decided to put a stop to this. He gave his brother James, the duke of York and Albany, the right to take over the Dutch colony.

In 1664, the duke sailed four warships into New Amsterdam's

The markets along
New York Harbor
around 1746

harbor. Stuyvesant urged his citizens to resist, but they knew they
didn't stand a chance. New Amsterdam surrendered quietly.

In honor of the duke, the colony was renamed New York, and
Fort Orange was called Albany. Life went on as usual under English rule. Farms and fruit orchards flourished in the river valleys,
while cattle, sheep, and horses grazed across the rolling hills.

### French and Indian Wars

Meanwhile, in the inland forests, the British and French competed
for the rich fur trade. French soldiers were building forts closer
and closer to the British colonies, and hostilities broke out from
time to time. In 1754, these conflicts exploded into the French and
Indian Wars.

In New York, major battles raged at Fort Niagara, Oswego, Fort William Henry, and Fort Ticonderoga. New settlers were afraid to move in to this hotbed, and settlement slowed down to a trickle. Both sides used Indians in the war. The Algonquins helped the French, while the Iroquois sided with the English. In 1763, England and France signed the Treaty of Paris, ending the wars and also confirming that New York belonged to England.

Now New York's population began to sky-rocket. Settlers poured in to farm along the Hudson River and deeper in the interior. By the 1780s, the New York colony was home to about 163,000 people.

Each year, hundreds of people visit the French castle at Old Fort Niagara.

## Rumblings of Another War

Throughout the colonies, some leaders were pushing for their own government in America. They were sick of living under England's laws, troops, and taxes. Calling themselves Patriots, they held meetings and led protests against the British. But other colonists, called Loyalists, were faithful to England. New Yorkers took positions, too, with thousands of people on each side.

In 1774, colonial leaders called together a Continental Congress. New York selected the lawyer John Jay as its representative. The delegates met in Philadelphia, Pennsylvania, to discuss how to deal with England and arrange some kind of self-rule. But the time for a peaceful solution soon ran out.

## The Revolution

In April 1775, the first shots of the American Revolution rang out. British troops and Massachusetts colonists exchanged fire, and eight American Patriots lay dead. Congress met again and named George Washington, a hero of the French and Indian War, as commander in chief of the Continental Army.

The conflict quickly spread throughout the colonies. Suspecting that the British would attack New York City, Washington moved his army there. While the troops were preparing to defend the city, a rider arrived with startling news.

On July 4, 1776, members of Congress had signed a Declaration of Independence. It declared that the thirteen colonies were now the thirteen United States of America. Washington's men broke out in cheers. Now they had more reason than ever to fight—for their own freedom in a country all their own.

On July 9, New Yorkers met in White Plains and approved the declaration. They also set up New York's own state government. Yet there was still much to do. Signing documents was one thing, but fighting a war of independence with the British was another. New York was the scene of almost one-third of the battles of the American Revolution.

On July 12, a British fleet of 150 warships sailed into New York Bay. In August, in the Battle of Long Island, the British took New York City. Other conflicts raged in the Hudson and Mohawk Valleys and along Lake Champlain.

The Battle of Freeman's Farm, north of Albany, was a turning point in the war. It ended with British general John Burgoyne's surrender to American general Horatio Gates at Saratoga (now

Schuylerville) in 1777. Hearing of the victory, France entered the war on the side of the Americans.

The surrender of Burgoyne's army at Saratoga

Farther west, meanwhile, the Iroquois were fighting under the British and attacking farming settlements. In retaliation, General Washington sent a force to demolish the Iroquois. Soldiers raided and burned Iroquois villages throughout the Mohawk Valley, the Finger Lakes region, and the Genesee Valley. This put an end to the once-powerful Iroquois Confederacy.

Things continued to go badly for the British. When Lord Cornwallis surrendered to General Washington in 1781, the war was over. Washington made his headquarters in Newburgh while he waited for a formal peace treaty to be signed. At one point, some of his officers offered him a crown. They felt he deserved to be king of the United States. Washington was indignant. "You could not have found a person to whom your schemes are more disagreeable," he replied.

After the peace treaty was signed in 1783, Washington marched triumphantly into New York City—the city he had lost to the British seven years before. Crowds cheered their beloved general and threw flowers in his path. In 1785, Congress chose New York City as the new nation's temporary capital. For the next five years, the U.S. government ruled from Federal Hall on Wall and Broad Streets.

## A New State in a New Nation

New Yorkers celebrating their ratification of the U.S. Constitution in 1789

Back in 1777, New Yorkers had drawn up their own state constitution. It was the first constitution in the nation. Yet the United States itself still had no governing document. New Yorker Alexander Hamilton helped organize a constitutional convention, which met in Philadelphia in 1787 and drew up a constitution. The next step was for all thirteen colonies to ratify it. Hamilton, John Jay, and James Madison wrote a set of powerful essays called *The Federalist Papers* to urge the colonies to vote their approval.

New Yorkers themselves

## Statehood—By a Three-Vote Margin

New York adopted a state constitution on April 20, 1777—twelve years before the United States had a constitution. Then New York's voters—male landowners—elected George Clinton as their first governor. On September 10, in the Kingston courthouse, the House of Assembly of the state of New York met for its first session.

But true statehood was still many years away. For the thirteen original colonies, statehood came only by ratifying the U.S. Constitution. New York delegates met in Poughkeepsie to vote on the constitution in June 1788. Things did not look good. Two-thirds of the delegates arrived at the meeting planning to vote no.

Then the news came that ten other colonies had voted for ratification. (Only nine were needed for the constitution to go into effect.) Now New Yorkers were afraid of losing trade with the other states. Some counties were even talking about pulling away from New York and joining other states. After debating bitterly for over a month, the delegates ratified the constitution by a vote of thirty to twenty-seven. ■

were divided about the constitution. Many were against the idea of a strong federal government. Stung by years of English rule, they wanted the states to have more power over their own affairs. Finally, on July 26, 1788, New York became the eleventh colony to ratify the U.S. Constitution. With that act, New York entered the union.

On April 30, 1789, George Washington stepped out onto the balcony of Federal Hall. Before him stretched a sea of wildly cheering citizens. Eventually, the noise died to a hush, and Washington took his oath of office as the first president of the United States of America.

**Washington being sworn in as the first president of the United States of America**

# CHAPTER THREE

# A Century of Progress

# The War of 1812

Troubles with Great Britain didn't end with the Revolution. In the early nineteenth century, British ships began stopping American ships on the high seas. Officers came aboard to search for British deserters. In the process, they sometimes forced American sailors into British service. At first, the United States reacted with an embargo, or a halt to all trade with England. But the embargo did no good, and in 1812, the United States declared war.

Governor De Witt Clinton and friends making their way by boat down the Erie Canal

Most New Yorkers were against the war. Merchants needed to trade with Great Britain to stay in business. Many of the battles, however, took place in New York. One decisive conflict took place on Lake Erie. In a valiant sea battle, Commodore Oliver Hazard Perry of the U.S. Navy won control of Lake Erie from the British. Then he sent to his superior the now-famous message: "We have met the enemy, and they are ours." Another turning point was the Battle of Lake Champlain, where Commodore Thomas Macdonough's gunboats drove off a British fleet. Peace came in December 1814, and again, life returned to normal.

## New Ways to Travel and Work

By the 1820s, settlers had cleared much of the state's land for farming. The Erie Canal opened in 1825. It had taken eight years to dig the "ditch" from the Hudson River to Lake Erie. Now farmers

Opposite: The Erie Canal at Lockport

## The Erie Canal

*I've got a mule, and her name is Sal—*
*Fifteen miles on the Erie Canal.*
*She's a good old worker and a good old pal—*
*Fifteen miles on the Erie Canal.*

Bargemen sang work songs like this one as their mules plodded alongside the canal pulling cargo-laden barges. Before the Erie Canal was built, it took weeks of travel over muddy, rocky roads to reach the Great Lakes from eastern New York.

In 1817, Governor De Witt Clinton convinced the legislature to spend $7 million to dig a canal from Albany on the Hudson River to Buffalo on Lake Erie. It would be 363 miles (584 km) long, 40 feet (12.2 m) wide, and 4 feet (1.2 m) deep. At first, New Yorkers called the idea "Clinton's Ditch" and "Clinton's Folly." But the ditch, opened in 1825, made a difference. Travel from the Atlantic Ocean, up the Hudson River, and through the canal to the Great Lakes was now possible. By 1840, New York City had become the busiest port in the nation. ■

could ship their crops on the waterways for export to the rest of the United States and to Europe.

Besides good waterways, the state had an extensive system of roads. Turnpikes ran along the Hudson and Mohawk Rivers and continued on to the west. They made life easier for pioneers, traders, and mail carriers. Horse-drawn wagons, stagecoaches, and covered wagons crowded the roads. Sheep and cattle farmers herded their animals to market on the turnpikes, too—it was much easier than winding through the woods.

Farming villages dotted the countryside, many with only a steepled church, a schoolhouse, and a general store. Carpenters and blacksmiths made farm equipment. At home, women at their spinning wheels spun cotton and wool for clothes. But machines were beginning to change the way people earned a living. Goods once made by hand could be mass-produced in factories. Soon New York's factories were making farm tools, woven cloth, and

iron and steel products. By 1850, New York was the top manufacturing state in the nation.

A Charles Codman landscape of New York country life around 1832

## A Time of Reforms

Many of New York's farmers were tenant farmers. They worked land that belonged to wealthy landowners and paid rent to use the land. In 1839, bitter farmers began harassing landowners and refusing to pay their rent. New laws in the 1840s finally gave small-scale farmers a chance to own their own land.

New Yorkers pushed for many other reforms in the 1830s and 1840s. The state abolished slavery and became a leader in the antislavery movement. One outspoken reformer was Horace Greeley. He wrote articles and lectured throughout the country on slavery and women's rights. Other reformers fought for the prohibition of liquor, labor reform, and a better life for the poor.

The Women's Rights National Historical Park in Seneca Falls honors the work of early New York reformers.

A Fourth of July parade honoring the New Yorkers who fought for the Union in the Civil War

New Yorkers Lucretia C. Mott and Elizabeth Cady Stanton championed women's right to vote. In 1848, they helped organize the first women's rights convention at Seneca Falls. Delegates issued a declaration demanding voting rights, educational opportunities, and equal treatment under the law.

## The Civil War

When the Civil War broke out in 1861, the U.S. government drafted men to fight against the Southern Confederates. But a man could pay $300 for a substitute to join the army in his place. In New York City, poor citizens and proslavery groups staged a riot against this system. In no time, the whole city was caught up in a frenzy of burning, looting, and killing. The Draft Riots of July 13–16, 1863, left 1,200 dead and 800 injured. Half a million New Yorkers fought on the Union side. One-tenth of them—50,000 people—died in the conflict.

After the war, the state's economy grew faster than ever and large companies became even bigger. Merchants turned to moneylenders on Wall Street for business loans. Wall Street grew until it became the financial capital of the world.

# Reformers

Horace Greeley (1811–1872) was a journalist and political leader (above left). He cofounded *The New Yorker* magazine in 1834 and founded the *New York Tribune* in 1841. Greeley swayed many Northerners to support the abolition of slavery. He also favored the Free Soil movement and pushed for universal public education. After the Civil War, he advocated voting rights for women and former slaves. He ran for president in 1872 but lost by a wide margin.

Julia Ward Howe (1819–1910), feminist and social reformer, was born in New York City, the daughter of a wealthy banker (above center). She fought for abolition and for women's right to vote. "The Battle Hymn of the Republic" is the best-known of her many poems. Howe founded the New England Woman Suffrage Association in 1868 and was the editor of *Woman's Journal* from 1870 to 1890.

St. Elizabeth Ann Seton (1774–1821) was the United States' first native-born Roman Catholic saint (above right). Born in New York City, she married a wealthy trader. In 1797, she founded the Society for the Relief of Poor Widows with Small Children. The mother of five children, she herself became a widow in 1803. She joined the Catholic Church and founded the Sisters of Charity, the first U.S. religious order. She was canonized as a saint in 1975. Her feast day is celebrated on January 4.

St. Frances (Francesca) Xavier Cabrini (1850–1917), born in Italy, was a Roman Catholic nun. In Italy, she founded the Missionary Sisters of the Sacred Heart. In 1889, she sailed to New York City, where she worked with the poor. An orphanage she founded is now known as the St. Cabrini Home in West Park. She became the first U.S. saint when she was canonized in 1946. Her feast day is November 13. ■

## New Yorkers Who Became U.S. President

**Martin Van Buren** (1782–1862) was the eighth president (1837–1841). He was born in Kinderhook, where he worked as a lawyer. Van Buren was a state senator (1813–1821), the state attorney general (1816–1819), a U.S. senator (1821–1828), and governor of New York (1828–1829). He went on to become U.S. secretary of state (1829-1831) and vice president under Andrew Jackson (1833–1837). Van Buren was then elected the next president.

**Millard Fillmore** (1800–1874) was the thirteenth president (1850–1853). He was born in Summer Hill and educated himself. Fillmore became a state assemblyman (1829), a U.S. congressman (1833), and New York State comptroller (1847). In 1849, he became vice president under President Zachary Taylor. When Taylor died in 1850, Fillmore moved up to the presidency.

**Chester Alan Arthur** (1830–1886) was the twenty-first president (1881–1885). Born in Vermont, he became a prominent lawyer and the Republican Party Leader in New York. Arthur was vice president under James Garfield. When Garfield was assassinated in his first year in office, Arthur became president.

**Grover Cleveland** (1837–1908) was the twenty-second and twenty-fourth president (1885–1889 and 1893–1897). Born in New Jersey, he worked as a lawyer in New York. Cleveland was elected mayor of Buffalo and then governor of the state.

**Theodore "Teddy" Roosevelt** (right) (1858–1919) was the twenty-sixth president (1901–1909). Born in New York City, he served as the president of the New York City Board of Police Commissioners and was elected to the state legislature in 1884. After leading his famous Rough Riders in the Spanish-American War, he became governor of New York (1898–1900). He was vice-president under William McKinley and became president when McKinley was assassinated. Roosevelt won the Nobel Peace Prize in 1906 for helping to end the Russo-Japanese War. He also pushed for construction of the Panama Canal and for social reforms. His cousin Franklin Delano Roosevelt, who was born in Hyde Park, became the thirty-second president. ■

Meanwhile, immigrants from Ireland, Germany, and other European countries poured into New York City by the thousands. They were willing to work long hours for whatever pay they could get. For many, this was better than the famines, wars, and persecutions they had left behind.

## Tammany Hall

In the mid-1800s, a powerful group of politicians controlled New York City. They belonged to a Democratic Party organization called Tammany Hall. Tammany began in 1789, when middle-class New Yorkers formed the Society of Tammany. They opposed the aristocratic Republican politicians who dominated the state after the American Revolution. As Irish immigration increased in the 1830s, Irishmen became Tammany's ringleaders.

In New York City, Tammany helped immigrants find jobs and become citizens. In return, people voted for Tammany candidates. This system was so efficient, it worked like a machine. Thus, it was called machine politics, or the Democratic machine. Leaders met in a building on 14th Street called Tammany Hall.

Powerful Tammany Hall bosses controlled city and even statewide elections. Because New York was the nation's most populous state, even presidential candidates tried to win the support of Tammany Hall.

## The Rise and Fall of Boss Tweed

Some Tammany Hall bosses worked to reform labor laws and improve working conditions in the city. Others were dishonest. With the help of the police, they forced gambling joints and other

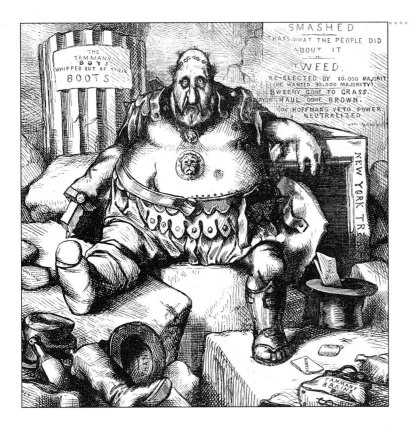

SMASHED
THAT'S WHAT THE PEOPLE DID ABOUT IT
TWEED.
RE-ELECTED BY 10,000 MAJORIT
(HE WANTED 30,000 MAJORITY)
SWEENY GONE TO GRASS.
MAYOR HAUL DONE BROWN.
GOV. HOFFMAN'S VETO POWER
NEUTRALIZED

THE TAMMANY BOYS WHIPPED OUT OF THEIR BOOTS

NEW YORK TR

**A famous Thomas Nast cartoon of Boss Tweed**

illegal operations to pay bribes, or "protection money." But William Marcy "Boss" Tweed was downright corrupt, and he made no effort to hide it.

As a modest city official, Tweed drew only a small salary. But he owned a Fifth Avenue town house and a lavish estate. How did he do it? By swindling millions of dollars from the city treasury. Cartoonist Thomas Nast was merciless in attacking Tweed and his cronies. Tweed was finally convicted and sent to jail, where he died in 1878.

Reformers in the Democratic Party tried to undo Tweed's damage. One was "Honest" John Kelly. Another reformer was a young police commissioner named Theodore Roosevelt. In 1894, the state legislature in Albany began hearings on Tammany Hall. But many years would pass before Tammany's power was broken.

### The Island of Tears

Until the 1890s, immigrants into New York arrived at Castle Garden. There they received information about the city's housing and social services. But in 1892, the U.S. government replaced Castle Garden with Ellis Island.

As a federal facility, Ellis Island screened newcomers to make

## Statue of Liberty National Monument

*Give me your tired, your poor,*
*Your huddled masses yearning to*
  *breathe free,*
*The wretched refuse of your*
  *teeming shore.*
*Send these, the homeless,*
  *tempest-tost to me,*
*I lift my lamp beside the golden*
  *door!*

Emma Lazarus's poem, inscribed beneath the Statue of Liberty, still grips the emotions today. The words embody what it meant for millions of immigrants to arrive in the United States. As they sailed toward New York Harbor, all eyes were fixed on the glistening statue. One Polish man said, "The bigness of Mrs. Liberty overcame us. No one spoke a word, for she was like a goddess [who represented] the country which was to be our future home."

A gift from the people of France, Lady Liberty was assembled on Liberty Island and dedicated in 1886. There are 189 steps to the top of its pedestal, 142 steps inside the statue to the head, and 54 ladder rungs up the arm that holds the torch.

Ellis Island in New York Bay opened as an immigration station in 1892. It handled only those immigrants who had traveled in a ship's cramped, foul-smelling steerage area below deck. (First- and second-class passengers were politely processed aboard ship.) More than 12 million people passed through the gates of Ellis Island before it closed in 1954. The island and the Statue of Liberty are now the Statue of Liberty National Monument. ■

**Ellis Island, as it looks today**

sure they fit in with U.S. immigration policies. Doctors examined them for diseases, and other officials sized them up. "Undesirables" were sent back home on another ten-day to one-month voyage. Because so many hopeful immigrants were turned away, Ellis Island came to be called the Island of Tears. Still, New York City's population grew from 1 million in 1860 to 3.4 million in 1900.

In the late nineteenth century, most new arrivals were Italians and Eastern European Jews. They swelled the slum tenements of Manhattan's Lower East Side, where thousands worked in clothing factories day and night, seven days a week. Many of the garment workers were women and children.

The crunch of people in Manhattan was so tight that many

homes and businesses spilled over into neighboring districts. The Brooklyn Bridge opened in 1883. It spanned the East River from Manhattan to Brooklyn. In 1898, the city's five boroughs—Manhattan, Brooklyn, Queens, the Bronx, and Staten Island—were joined as one city.

## The Triangle Shirtwaist Company Fire

Working conditions in New York's garment factories were frightful and unsafe. Disaster struck on a Saturday afternoon in 1911, when the Triangle Shirtwaist Company went up in flames. It occupied the eighth, ninth, and tenth floors of a building in Washington Square. Most of the employees were Italian and Jewish women and girls between the ages of thirteen and twenty-three.

In less than fifteen minutes, the entire company burned and 146 people died. Most were trapped inside the blazing building, while others jumped from the windows to their death. The disaster led the state to pass a series of labor laws, including fire safety codes, child labor laws, and workers' compensation laws. ■

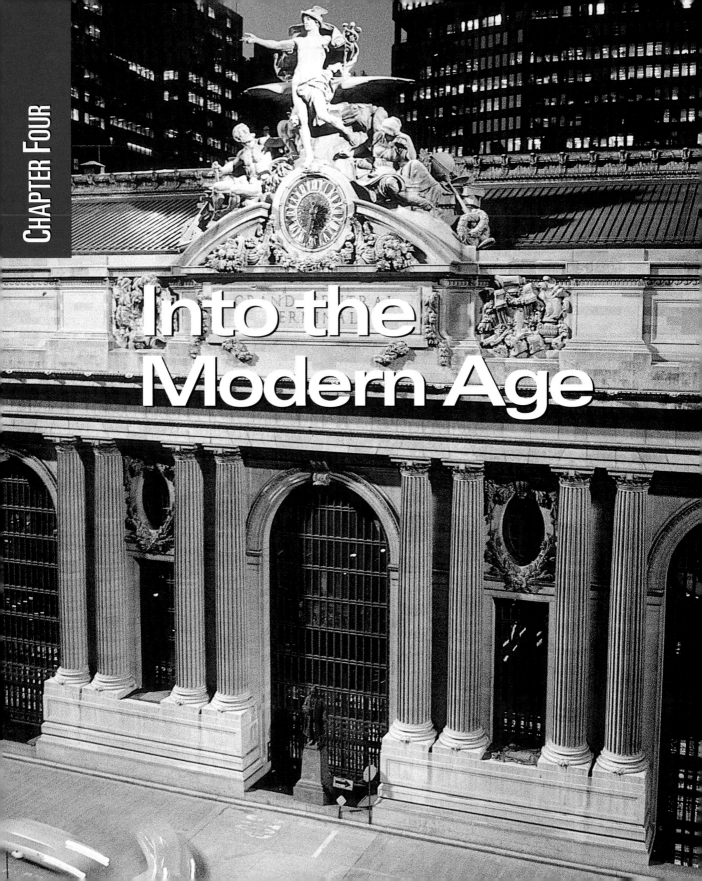

# CHAPTER FOUR

# Into the Modern Age

"Let us ever remember that our interest is in concord, not conflict. And that our real eminence rests in the victories of peace, not those of war."

With these inspiring words, President William McKinley addressed the crowds at the 1901 Pan-American Exposition in Buffalo, New York. He urged that a canal be built across Panama and a telegraph cable be laid across the Pacific. They would, he hoped, bring people of the world closer together in peace. The next day, an anarchist named Leon Czolgosz shot McKinley point-blank on the exposition grounds. He died a week later.

Vice President Theodore Roosevelt—New York City's former police commissioner—was sworn in as president. Conservation was one of Roosevelt's major interests. As president, he set aside millions of acres of forestland as national forests and parks. And he began the construction of the Panama Canal.

**President William McKinley**

## High Society in the Gilded Age

In the early 1900s, wealthy New York industrialists reigned from their offices on Wall Street. Their gigantic corporations, called trusts, had grown till they controlled much of the nation's railroad, oil, and banking industries.

For New York's upper crust, this was the Gilded Age, or Golden Age. It lasted from the 1890s into the 1920s. Millionaires lived in elegant mansions and town houses on Fifth Avenue. Their evenings

**Opposite: New York City's Grand Central Station**

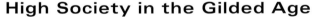

## Leading Families of the Gilded Age

**John Pierpont (J. P.) Morgan** (1837–1913) was a banker and philanthropist. His banking firm was one of the most powerful in the world. In 1901, he formed the United States Steel Corporation. Morgan gave away large sums of money to charity, including major contributions to the Metropolitan Museum of Art. He left his collection of books and drawings to the Morgan Library, which is housed in his former mansion.

**John Davison Rockefeller** (1839–1937) was born in Richford. In 1875, he and his brother William founded the Standard Oil Company. The company was severely criticized for controlling the U.S. oil trade. Rockefeller donated over $500 million to universities and medical researchers. He established the Rockefeller Foundation in 1913. His son John Jr. (1874–1960) built Manhattan's Rockefeller Center.

**John Jacob Astor** (1763–1848) was born in Germany. At age twenty-one, he sailed to New York City and started the America Fur Company. In 1811, he founded a settlement called Astoria in what is today Oregon. He willed money to New York City for a public library. His great-grandson, John Jacob Astor (1864–1912), helped build New York City's Waldorf-Astoria Hotel. He died on the voyage of the ill-fated Titanic.

**Jason (Jay) Gould** (1836–1892) was born in Roxbury, New York. He became the major shareholder of a bank in Pennsylvania and director of the Erie Railway Company.

**Cornelius Vanderbilt** (1794–1877) was born in a poor family on Staten Island. At sixteen, he bought his own boat and began giving ferry rides between New York City and Staten Island. By age forty, he owned a great fleet of steamships that traveled up the Hudson. Later, he invested in several railroad companies. He donated the money to build Vanderbilt University in Nashville, Tennessee. ■

## Hot Times in Harlem

Harlem was a hotbed of black culture in the 1920s and 1930s. It was the Jazz Age, and both black and white audiences packed Harlem's jazz clubs. The most famous spot was the Cotton Club. It featured Billie Holiday, Duke Ellington, Count Basie, Cab Calloway, and other jazz greats of the day. Meanwhile, black writers, political leaders, and social reformers formed a movement called the Harlem Renaissance. ■

were filled with glamorous social events. For the summer, they retreated to huge estates in upstate New York. Parties there could last a week or more.

The queen of New York's high society was Caroline Astor. She developed a list called the Four Hundred—that is, the four hundred people worthy of being invited to one of her balls. Why four hundred? Because, she explained, her "modest" ballroom could hold only four hundred people!

New York City charged ahead with new subways, skyscrapers, and massive train stations. Pennsylvania Station opened in 1910. Cornelius Vanderbilt built the original Grand Central Depot in 1871 as the endpoint of his New York Central Railroad. The present-day Grand Central was dedicated in 1913.

Democrat Alfred E. Smith was New York's governor for most of the 1920s. Though he was a Tammany Hall candidate, he pushed for labor reforms and aid to the poor. He ran for president in 1928 but lost to Herbert Hoover. Smith was the first Roman Catholic to run for president.

Food being distributed to the poor and hungry during the Great Depression

## The Crash and the Depression Years

By the 1920s, the New York Stock Exchange on Wall Street handled billions of dollars' worth of business a day. Then came Black Tuesday—October 29, 1929. The stock market crashed, businesses failed, banks closed, and millions of people across the country lost all they owned. This began the nation's Great Depression.

In New York City, hungry people lined up at soup kitchens to get a bite to eat. On street corners, ragged adults and children sold apples, pencils, flowers—anything to earn a few pennies.

Some common laborers and skilled artisans continued working during the depression. They completed construction of some of New York City's most beautiful and famous buildings. The Chrysler Building opened in 1930 and the Empire State Building in 1931. The gigantic Rockefeller Center complex went up between 1931 and 1940.

In the early 1930s, the state-appointed Seabury Commission investigated Tammany Hall. It found an intricate network of corruption throughout New York City. This included Mayor Jimmy Walker, Tammany district leaders, the police, and criminals such as bootleggers. Everyone was making a lot of money from illegal payoffs. After Walker resigned, Tammany Hall's power was broken at last.

The next mayor, Fiorello La Guardia (1882–1947), was a colorful and beloved figure. His nickname was the Little Flower, from his Italian first name. "No more free lunch!" was his approach to the leftovers of Tammany Hall. He fought corruption, reorganized city government, cleaned up slums, and added parks and playgrounds to the city.

Franklin D. Roosevelt, a fifth cousin of Theodore, became New York's governor in 1929. He set up social programs to help the state's depression-stricken citizens. It was a good training ground for Roosevelt's next challenge.

## The Roosevelt Presidency

Roosevelt became president in 1933. He had to help an entire nation rise up out of the depression. He set up a program called the New Deal, modeled after policies that had worked in New York. It included jobs, welfare programs for the needy, and a social security system for retired people.

### Franklin Delano Roosevelt

Franklin Delano Roosevelt (1882–1945) was the thirty-second U.S. president (1933–1945). Born in Hyde Park, he was a state senator (1910–1913), assistant secretary of the U.S. Navy (1913–1920), and governor of New York (1929–1932). Roosevelt became crippled with polio in 1921 but always tried to hide his condition from the public. As president, he instituted his New Deal policies to help the nation recover from the Great Depression. Roosevelt brought the United States into World War II and worked on peace negotiations but died just before the war ended. He was the only president to be elected four times. ■

Roosevelt faced an even greater challenge when World War II (1939–1945) broke out. In 1941, the Japanese bombed U.S. military bases in Pearl Harbor, Hawaii. Under Roosevelt's leadership, the United States immediately entered the war.

During the war, half the nation's fighting force shipped out of New York Harbor to fight in Europe. New York's factories went into high gear turning out ammunition, vehicles, and other war supplies. This benefited cities such as Buffalo, Rochester, and Syracuse.

## Postwar Progress

After the war, fifty nations around the world joined together to form the United Nations. They chose New York City as their permanent headquarters. John D. Rockefeller Jr. donated a tract of land along the East River for the building. In 1952, the U.N. Headquarters was completed.

**The United Nations building**

Waterways, highways, and bridges went up all over the state while Nelson Rockefeller was governor (1959–1973). After the St. Lawrence Seaway opened in 1959, New York's ports on Lake Ontario and Lake Erie became ports for Atlantic Ocean ships. The next year, highway crews completed the New York State Thruway (renamed the Thomas E. Dewey Thruway in 1964).

In the 1960s, Lincoln Center for the Performing Arts opened in Manhattan, and Empire State Plaza went up in Albany. The twin towers of the World Trade Center opened in 1974.

But the 1970s were a rough time for upstate industrial towns. Over half a million people left the state when factories closed. The 1970s also brought wars and other political upheavals in Southeast Asia and Latin America. For New York, this meant that most immigrants were now Asian and Hispanic people.

## Modern Concerns

Environmental issues were a priority in the 1980s. Hazardous wastes from factories were causing health problems. Love Canal near Niagara Falls was found to be especially dangerous. Horrified by the contamination, voters approved massive funds to clean up waste sites around the state.

New York politicians made the headlines in the 1980s. In 1984, the Democratic Party nominated Geraldine Ferraro as its vice presidential candidate. The congresswoman from Queens was the first female from a major party to run for national office. Meanwhile, New York City's colorful mayor Edward Koch led the city out of bankruptcy. In 1993, Rudolph Giuliani was elected mayor. His efforts to clean up the city have been praised by many.

Today, New York faces many of the same problems that other states do—improving schools, repairing highways, providing social services for the poor, and combating crime. Yet New York remains a shining star in the world community. As the seat of the United Nations and the world center for finance, fashion, and the arts, New York leads the way to the twenty-first century.

Geraldine Ferraro addressing the crowd at the 1984 Democratic National Convention

# CHAPTER FIVE

# New York in the Wild

**D**uring the Ice Age—more than 10,000 years ago—glaciers covered most of New York. They gouged out the valleys where New York's rivers now run. Where mountains and hills jutted up, glaciers smoothed and rounded their peaks.

A magnificent view of the Hudson River and highlands

As the earth warmed, the glaciers began to melt, leaving mineral-rich sediment behind. Sediment composed of the mineral lime now forms New York's richest farmland; it settled all across the state, but the deepest deposits drifted into the lake beds and river valleys.

## The Hudson and Mohawk River Valleys

The Hudson River rises in the Adirondack Mountains in northeastern New York. It flows south all the way to New York Bay, where it empties into the Atlantic Ocean. About halfway along its course is Albany, the state capital.

The Mohawk River, the Hudson's main branch, splits off just north of Albany. New York's early pioneers settled along these

Opposite: Looking south from Snowy Mountain in Adirondack Park

New York in the Wild **47**

## Putting New York in Its Place

New York is one of the three Middle Atlantic states. The other two—New Jersey and Pennsylvania—border New York to the south. Along New York's eastern border are three New England states—Vermont, Massachusetts, and Connecticut. On the west are Lake Erie, a small piece of Pennsylvania, and the Niagara River. Just across the river is the Canadian province of Ontario. Most of New York's northern border consists of water—Lake Ontario and the St. Lawrence River, with Ontario on the other side. New York's northernmost boundary is a straight line, which separates New York and Canada's province of Quebec. ■

two rivers. Naturally, the Hudson and Mohawk became the territory's main transportation routes.

The Erie Canal, opened in 1825, ran even farther west than the Mohawk. It stretched across the state from Albany on the Hudson to Buffalo on Lake Erie. Cities such as Buffalo, Rochester, and Syracuse grew up as manufacturing and shipping centers along the canal.

## The New England Uplands and the Atlantic Coastal Plain

A long strip of eastern New York is called the New England Uplands. It includes the Taconic Mountains that rise east of the Hudson Valley. New York shares this mountain range with the New England states of Vermont, Massachusetts, and Connecticut. The uplands continue across the mouth of the Hudson and into Pennsylvania.

This region encompasses two of the five boroughs that make up New York City—Manhattan and the Bronx. The other three boroughs—Staten Island, Brooklyn, and Queens—are part of the Atlantic Coastal Plain.

The Atlantic Coastal Plain runs all the way down the U.S. east

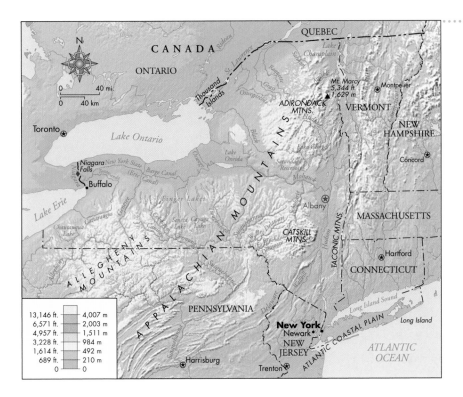

**Topographical map of New York**

coast from Massachusetts to Florida. In New York, only Long Island and Staten Island belong to this region. Vegetable and dairy farms, greenhouses, and plant nurseries thrive here. Long Island is just that—a long island stretching out into the Atlantic Ocean. Brooklyn and Queens are on its western end.

## The Appalachian Highlands

West of the Hudson are the Catskill Mountains. They're part of New York's Appalachian Highlands region, which covers about half the state. This region belongs to the massive Appalachian Mountain system that runs through eastern North America from Canada to Alabama. In New York, the highlands extend from the Hudson Valley all the way through central and southern New York. Another

## New York's Geographical Features

| | |
|---|---|
| **Total area; rank** | 53,989 sq. mi. (139,831 sq km); 27th |
| **Land; rank** | 47,224 sq. mi. (122,310 sq km); 30th |
| **Water; rank** | 6,765 sq. mi. (17,521 sq km); 5th |
| *Inland water; rank* | 1,888 sq. mi. (4,890 sq km); 10th |
| *Coastal water; rank* | 976 sq. mi. (2,528 sq km); 8th |
| *Great Lakes water; rank* | 3,901 sq. mi. (10,104 sq km); 3rd |
| **Geographic center** | Madison, 12 miles (19 km) south of Oneida and 26 miles (42 km) southwest of Utica |
| **Highest point** | Mount Marcy, 5,344 feet (1,629 m) |
| **Lowest point** | Sea level at the Atlantic Ocean |
| **Largest city** | New York City |
| **Population; rank** | 18,044,505 (1990 census); 2nd |
| **Record high temperature** | 108°F (42°C) at Troy on July 22, 1926 |
| **Record low temperature** | –52°F (–47°C) at Old Forge on February 18, 1979 |
| **Average July temperature** | 69°F (21°C) |
| **Average January temperature** | 21°F (–6°C) |
| **Average annual precipitation** | 39 inches (99 cm) |

name for the region is the Allegheny Plateau. The name comes from the Allegheny Mountains, one of the ranges in the Appalachian Mountain system.

Within the Appalachian Highlands are the Catskills, the Finger Lakes, and several river valleys. The Catskills region is a popular year-round recreation area. In its river valleys, farmers raise grapes, fruit trees, and vegetables. The Finger Lakes of north-central New York are eleven long, thin lakes. The two largest are Lake Seneca and Lake Cayuga. This region, too, attracts vacationers year-round. Dairy farms thrive on the level grasslands between the lakes.

**Lake Placid village along Mirror Lake**

## The Adirondacks

Just north of the Mohawk Valley are the Adirondacks. These rugged and beautiful mountains cover most of northeastern New York. Resorts and recreation areas are scattered throughout the Adirondacks. But only hardy adventurers spend time in the wildest regions of the north, called the North Woods. Much of the Adirondacks region is a state-protected wilderness reserve called Adirondack Park. Covering about 9,000 square miles (23,310 sq km), the park is almost as large as Vermont or New Hampshire.

Mount Marcy, New York's highest point, is one of many tall peaks in the Adirondacks. The next highest are Algonquin Peak and Haystack Mountain. Streams cascade into waterfalls as they rush down the mountainsides. About 2,000 lakes sparkle among the forested mountains and hills. Lakes Placid, Saranac, Tupper, and Long are some of the largest. Lake Champlain, on the New York–Vermont border, continues into Canada.

## Northern Waterways

In New York's far north, the Adirondacks slope down toward the St. Lawrence River. For part of its course, the St. Lawrence separates New York from the Canadian province of Ontario. The rolling

**Niagara Falls on the U.S. side**

lowlands of the river valley are dotted with dairy farms and fruit tree orchards. Near Kingston, the St. Lawrence widens around the Thousand Islands. There are really 1,793 islands in this group. Some belong to Ontario, and others belong to New York.

Two of North America's Great Lakes—Lake Erie and Lake Ontario—form much of New York's northern border. Land along the lakeshore is ideal for growing fruit trees. From ports on the Great Lakes, early New Yorkers could ship their goods to the western United States. Sailing east, ships could go into the St. Lawrence Seaway and on to the Atlantic Ocean.

## Rivers

The Niagara River, at New York's western tip, connects the two Great Lakes. It's only 36 miles (58 km) long. As it plunges over a steep ridge into the gorge below, it creates Niagara Falls—one of the most famous waterfalls in the world. Niagara Falls spans the U.S.–Canadian border. In the U.S. section are the American Falls and Bridal Veil Falls.

The Delaware River flows out of the Catskills and forms part of New York's border with Pennsylvania. Much of New York City's water supply comes from the Delaware. The Susquehanna River rises in Otsego Lake and flows south into Pennsylvania. Binghamton, in south-central New York, is the major town along its course. The Genesee River is the main river of western New York. Coming from Pennsylvania, it flows north through the state and empties into Lake Ontario.

## Trees and Flowers

Forests cover more than half of New York. Most of the state's 150 tree species are northern varieties. But a few—such as sweet gums and tulip trees—are native to the southern United States. The Adirondack Mountains are thickly wooded with cone-bearing evergreens such as pine and spruce. Mixed in with them are hard-

Giant sugar maples along Lake Champlain

woods such as beech and sugar maple trees. Delicious maple syrup comes from the sugar maple, New York's state tree. Forests are scattered across the broad Appalachian Plateau, too. Ash, birch, cherry, and oak trees are some other species in the mountains and hills. Oaks dominate the woodlands of southeastern New York.

Beautiful wildflowers blanket the hillsides in the springtime. Daisies, black-eyed Susans, and devil's paintbrush set the river valleys ablaze with color. Buttercups, violets, and clover carpet acres of meadows. Goldenrod and wild rose—the state flower—cluster at the edges of the woods. Deep in the forests' dappled shade grow Indian pipe, trillium, goldthread, and bunchberry.

## Animals

Black bears live in New York's mountains, and white-tailed deer roam the forests. Beavers, long hunted for their fur, still make their homes near rivers and streams. The sound of rustling leaves on the forest floor may signal the presence of small mammals. Raccoons, woodchucks, red foxes, opossums, and skunks have skittered through New York's forests for ages.

Snowshoe hares inhabit the high northern regions, while cottontail rabbits hop through lower woods and fields. Red squirrels, gray squirrels, and black squirrels scamper through forests, city parks, and backyards throughout the state.

Many more animal species used to inhabit New York's woodlands. But mountain lions and timber wolves have almost disappeared. Some species dwindled from hunting and trapping, and others declined because their natural habitats were cleared. Otters and minks were once vanishing from New York, too. But wildlife managers began reintroducing them in the 1990s.

Some birds live in New York year-round. They include black-capped titmice, gold-

**A white-tailed deer in Adirondack Park**

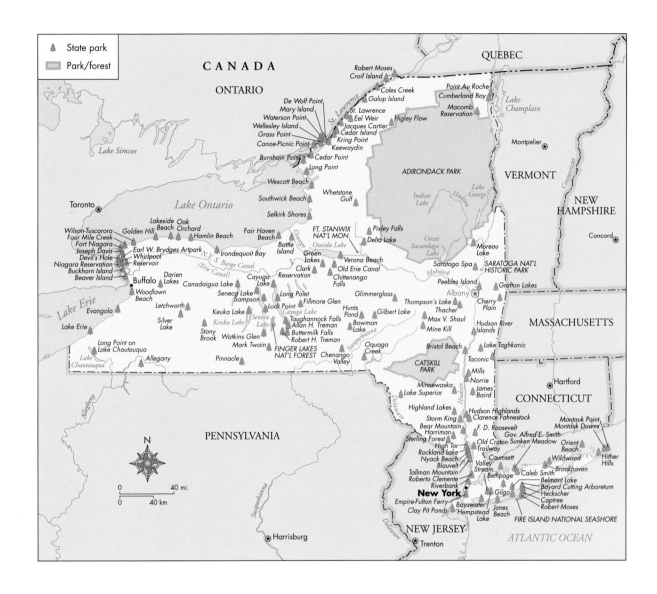

New York's parks and forests

finches, waxwings, sparrows, woodpeckers, crows, and hawks. Others fly south for the winter but spend spring and summer in New York. One is the bluebird, New York's state bird. Other summer visitors are robins, thrushes, and wrens.

## The Year of Seasons

"It freezes and snows severely in winter," one of New York's early settlers complained.

Nearly 300 years later, New Yorkers still grumble when winter settles in. Buffalo, Rochester, and Syracuse get more snow than any other big cities in the country. The Tug Hill Plateau, southwest of the Adirondacks, is unusually snowy, too. More snow falls there than anywhere else in the country east of the Rocky Mountains.

Not everyone complains of the snowy weather, though. Heavy snows in the Catskills and the Adirondacks are great opportunities for bobsledding and skiing. And in the North Woods, glistening mounds of snow on the pine branches are an enchanting sight.

Bus delays are normal during the winters in Syracuse.

Average temperatures in January range from 33°F (1°C) on Long Island to 14°F (–10°C) in the Adirondacks. When the mountain snows melt in the spring, rivers swell and gush. Apple trees in the lowlands are in bloom, and wildflowers cover the rolling hills.

Summer brings sun lovers out to the beaches and sea-shores. Manhattan's Central Park fills with bicyclers and roller skaters. Dogs chase Frisbees, and office workers sun-bathe on their lunch hours. In

July, Long Island's average temperature is a pleasant 74°F (23°C). But high in the Adirondacks, the midsummer average is only 66°F (19°C).

**Central Park in spring**

In autumn, the air is crisp, and maple trees turn brilliant shades of yellow and red. This is a time when many out-of-staters like to take driving trips through New York.

In much of New York, people live under cloudy skies more often than sunny skies. That's because moisture gathers over the Great Lakes and forms huge clouds that drift over the state. In Binghamton, the sky is totally clear for an average of only sixty-eight days a year!

# CHAPTER SIX

# Come on a Journey

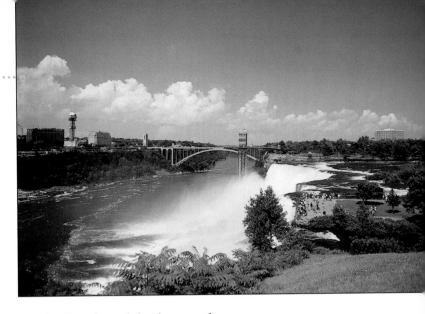

**The American Falls**

**B**uffalo, in far-western New York, is the state's second-largest city. Water made Buffalo a thriving and prosperous city. It sits at the eastern edge of Lake Erie and at the start of the Niagara River. To the north is the end of the Erie Canal, and farther north is Lake Ontario, the gateway to the St. Lawrence Seaway and the Atlantic Ocean. Once the Erie Canal opened, Great Lakes steamboats pulled into Buffalo loaded with settlers and freight.

In Buffalo's Gilded Age, the wealthy class lived in elegant mansions on Millionaires' Row. One of these, the Wilcox Mansion, is now the Theodore Roosevelt Inaugural National Historic Site. Here, in 1901, Roosevelt was sworn in as president after William McKinley was assassinated. The tall spire of the McKinley Monument stands before city hall. Built in the Art Deco style of the 1930s, city hall offers a great view of the city and its waterways.

Buffalo's millionaires spent elegant evenings at the theater. Many of those ornate theaters, now renovated, still line the theater district on Main Street.

In the nineteenth century, Niagara Falls was a favorite destination for vacationers and honeymooners. Now, with over 12 million visitors a year, it's as popular as ever. More than 500,000 gallons (2.2 million l) of water cascade over the cliffs every second. On the U.S. side are American Falls and Bridal Veil Falls, while Horseshoe Falls belongs to Canada. Between them is Goat Island. Visitors can

**Opposite: The Lake Erie Basin in Buffalo**

An aerial view of old Fort Niagara on Lake Ontario in Youngstown

take an elevator from the island to the foot of the falls. There a wooden walkway leads right up to the crashing torrent.

Fort Niagara overlooks the point where the Niagara River meets Lake Ontario. The fort was a hot spot during the French and Indian Wars, the American Revolution, and the War of 1812. Now, in the summertime, troops stage reenactments of some of the major battles of that time.

What was it like to ride a barge on the Erie Canal? Mule-drawn barge cruises from Medina take passengers back to the 1830s, while banjo players sing tunes from the canal days.

Acres of grapevines line Lake Erie in far-western New York. The lake air and rich soil make perfect conditions for growing wine grapes. A few miles inland, the Chautauqua Institution rests along the bank of Chautauqua Lake. In the 1870s, Sunday school teachers strolled the wooded grounds during summer studies there. Later, it was a summer resort offering music, dance, and other cultural shows. Chautauqua is still a popular retreat for taking in classes, concerts, plays, and art exhibits.

East of Chautauqua Lake is Conewango Amish Village. This place seems to be frozen in a quieter, simpler time. Villagers travel in horse-drawn buggies, and bearded farmers walk their furrowed rows behind horse-drawn plows. Residents sell the many fruits of their labor—handmade furniture, hand-sewn quilts, and homemade bread and cheese.

An Amish farmer and his draft horses in Conewango Amish Village

Farther east is Allegany State Park, adjoining Pennsylvania's Allegheny National Forest. Surrounding this wilderness area is Allegany Indian Reservation. It's the territory of New York's Seneca Indians, known as the Keepers of the Western Door of the Iroquois Confederacy. Exhibits in the Seneca-Iroquois Museum portray the Senecas' culture, heritage, and traditional way of life.

## Central New York and the Finger Lakes

Rochester is perched on the Genesee River near its mouth on Lake Ontario. It was an important port on the Erie Canal, too. As a shipping and manufacturing hub for central New York, Rochester grew to be the state's third-largest city. Italian, German, Polish, Irish, and Canadian people helped build its industries.

In Brown's Race Historic District, visitors admire the High Falls of the Genesee River. On summer evenings, the falls light up with a dazzling laser and fireworks show.

Rochester's most famous resident was George Eastman, inventor of the Kodak camera. His fifty-room mansion on East Avenue is now a museum. Next door is the International Museum of Photography. It shows many of the earliest photos and movies ever made.

Susan B. Anthony's Rochester home was the center for her fight for women's voting rights. Her home in Rochester, where she was arrested for voting, is now a museum. Another Rochester home, the Margaret

A view of the George Eastman residence from the east terrace garden

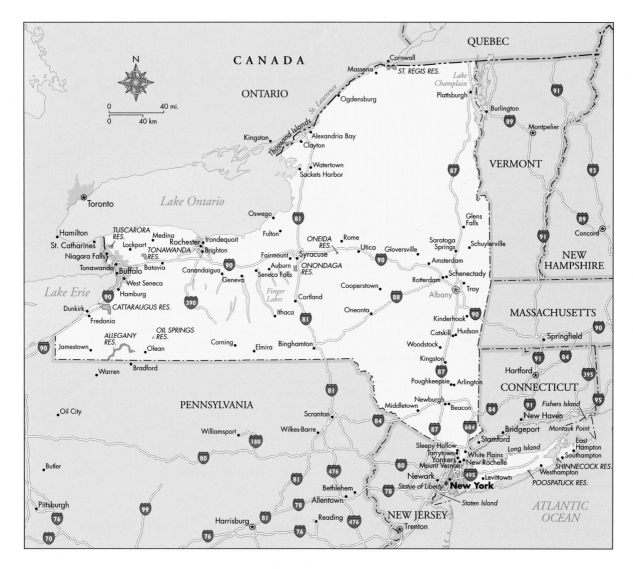

**New York's cities and interstates**

Woodbury Strong Museum, is filled with thousands of dolls, dollhouses, and other collections.

At Genesee Country Village in Mumford, just outside of Rochester, country roads lead to pioneer farms and Victorian mansions. Visitors can stop in at a log cabin, join a family as they prepare a meal, help with the village chores, or dance a jig at a hoedown.

Farther up the Genesee River is Letchworth State Park. Its showpiece is the 600-foot (183-m) Genesee River Gorge. Three waterfalls plunge down its rocky walls, and whitewater rafters get hair-raising thrill rides.

The long, thin Finger Lakes stretch out across the center of the state. For the Iroquois, this was where the Great Spirit laid his hand upon the earth. Between the lakes, the rolling hills are carpeted with farms and vineyards. Pleasure boaters can spend all day cruising beautiful Seneca Lake, 35 miles (56 km) long. At its southern end is Watkins Glen State Park. For a workout, hikers take the narrow Gorge Trail to the high cliff tops.

Near the north end of Seneca Lake is Seneca Falls. Seneca Falls is called the birthplace of women's rights. Here, in 1848, leaders of the women's movement held the Seneca Falls Convention, the first women's rights convention. The Women's Rights National Historical Park traces the movement with films, exhibits, and guided tours. The National Women's Hall of Fame celebrates extraordinary women of the past and present.

In nearby Auburn is the home of Harriet Tubman. An escaped slave, Tubman helped hundreds of other slaves gain their freedom. The next town to the east is Skaneateles. Residents love to tell visitors how to pronounce the name—Skinny Atlas! Located on the northern shore of Skaneateles Lake, this is a pleasant resort town of boutiques and cafés.

**The Genesee River gorge**

In Corning, south of Seneca Lake, the Corning Glass Center includes a museum of glassware and the Steuben glassmaking factory. Mark Twain had close ties to Elmira, east of Corning. He wrote *The Adventures Huckleberry Finn* on the Elmira College campus. He met his wife, Olivia Langdon, in Elmira, and he's buried in Elmira's Woodlawn Cemetery.

At the southern end of Cayuga Lake is Ithaca, home of Cornell University. Beautifully laid out on wooded hills, the campus is home to over 20,000 students.

## The Hudson River Valley

State Line Lookout is a great place to begin a trip into the Hudson Valley. Perched up high on the New York–New Jersey border, it offers a sweeping view of New York State's two worlds. To the south is Manhattan, and to the north is the Hudson Valley. Here, at the southern end of the Hudson, the west bank is lined with a sheer wall of cliffs called the Palisades. Henry Hudson must have been awestruck as he sailed upriver in their shadow.

Across the river around Tarrytown are the homes of some famous New Yorkers. One is Lyndhurst, the castlelike mansion of financier Jay Gould. Another is Sunnyside, the country home of Washington Irving. "The Legend of Sleepy Hollow," "Rip Van Winkle," and many other enchanting tales are set in the hills and valleys that Irving himself loved to explore.

Irving is buried in the nearby town of Sleepy Hollow. Next to the cemetery is a Dutch church where locals believed a headless ghost once lurked. That gave Irving the idea for his tale of the headless horseman.

The upper mills of Sleepy Hollow's Philipsburg Manor

Sleepy Hollow's Philipsburg Manor was the home of the eighteenth-century Dutch trader Frederick Philipse. He had been one of the landowners under the patroon system. Visitors can see his stone manor house, grist mill, and farm with costumed guides. Nearby is Kykuit, the summer home of John D. Rockefeller and his descendants. Within the six-story mansion is a collection of modern art and sculpture. Surrounding the house are formal gardens with marble fountains.

Farther up the river valley is Bear Mountain State Park. In the autumn, the park is ablaze with brilliantly colored foliage. From atop Bear Mountain, visitors can gaze north into the Hudson Highlands. In this wild and rugged stretch of the Hudson, steep mountainsides flank the river on both sides. Painters of the Hudson River School found a special challenge in trying to capture the highlands' dark and brooding atmosphere.

One high spot for surveying the river is Trophy Point. It's on the grounds of the United States Military Academy at West Point. Ulysses S. Grant, Robert E. Lee, Douglas MacArthur, and Dwight D. Eisenhower are just a few of its famous graduates. Visitors are welcome to tour the campus and its military museum and watch uniformed cadets on parade.

Graduation at the U.S. Military Academy at West Point

Farther north, in Newburgh, is Washington's Headquarters State Historic Site. Across the river, Mount Beacon perches on the Hudson's east bank. Patriots lit beacon fires here to alert Washington when British troops were on the move.

For kids in the nineteenth century, sticky saltwater taffy was a favorite treat. Kids today can get some at the general store in Museum Village. In this open-air museum in Orange County, an old-time nineteenth-century village goes about its daily life.

Vassar College was built in Poughkeepsie in 1881. Among the thousands of works in its art museum are paintings by artists of the Hudson River school.

In Hyde Park, north of Poughkeepsie, stand three remarkable homes. The fifty-four-room Vanderbilt Mansion is a typical "palace" of New York's Gilded Age, with tall columns, splendid interior, and acres of grounds. The Franklin D. Roosevelt National Historic Site is the home where Roosevelt grew up. It was also a summer White House, where he entertained important diplomats. Val-Kill, Eleanor Roosevelt's private retreat, is another historic site.

Artist Thomas Cole painted scenes of the Hudson Valley and the Catskills from his studio in Catskill. Olana, the exotic villa of Cole's student, Frederic Church, stands across the river near Hudson. Visitors are welcome to hike and ski there.

**The wagon-maker's shop at the Museum Village in Orange County**

## The Catskills and Beyond

Artists of the Hudson River School loved to paint the mountains, valleys, and waterfalls of the Catskills. One of their favorite sites was Kaaterskill Falls. Much of the region's unspoiled wilderness is protected as Catskill Park and Forest Preserve.

Weary of city life, vacationers head up to the Catskills to fish, swim, golf, hike, and ski. The region is dotted with resorts, motels, and camping sites. Luxury resorts offer top nightclub entertainment, as well as beautiful scenery.

The National Baseball Hall of Fame is the major attraction in Cooperstown. Visitors can learn just about anything about baseball on its computer screens, or they can gaze at relics of the past, such as Babe Ruth's ball and bat used for his sixtieth home run.

The Farmers Museum in Cooperstown is an open-air museum that recreates New York life from around 1790 to 1860. Spinners, weavers, a blacksmith, a broom maker, and others ply their trades in costumes and settings of the period. Fenimore House Museum, across the street, was once the home of writer James Fenimore Cooper.

Woodstock is still an artists' and hippies' colony, just as it was in the 1960s. A farm outside of Bethel was the scene of the legendary Woodstock Festival in the summer of 1969.

**National Baseball Hall of Fame**

The Saratoga Race
Track in Saratoga
Springs

## Albany and the Upper Hudson Valley

The state capitol in Albany took thirty-one years (1867–1898) to complete. It's a magnificent combination of Italian and French Renaissance as well as Romanesque styles. Stone-carved faces and animals peek out from the pillars and walls. The ornately carved western stairway is called the Million Dollar Staircase. Up the hill from the capitol is the Empire State Plaza. On one side is the huge, ultramodern performing arts center called the Egg.

Albany's New York State Museum is the oldest and largest state museum in the country. Exhibits on the Iroquois and other Native American peoples include life-size scenes, as well as audio and video programs. In its geology collection are samples of 20,000 rocks and minerals found in the state.

Three historic homes in Albany are now museums—the Ten Broeck Mansion, Cherry Hill Mansion, and the Schuyler Mansion. All three were built by prominent Dutch citizens in the 1700s.

Crailo State Historic Site in Rensselaer, built in 1642, is one of the few Dutch manor houses remaining from the days of the patroonships. It's now a museum of Hudson Valley Dutch culture. Saratoga Springs is a historic resort town famous for its horse racing, healthful mineral springs, and performing arts. New Skete Monastery in Cambridge is an Eastern Orthodox monastery set in the wilderness. Visitors can view its wood carvings and icons and shop for foods made there.

## The Adirondacks

"Forever wild"—that's the way 40 percent of Adirondack Park shall remain, according to a state law of 1892. The park covers about 6 million acres (2.4 million ha) of the Adirondacks' Mountains, forests, lakes, and streams. Hiking trails and campgrounds make it easy for visitors to enjoy this scenic wilderness.

The High Peaks region is the most rugged part of the Adirondacks. Among its many peaks is Mount Marcy, the state's highest point. Rivers and streams rush down the mountainsides, and their waters gather into hundreds of lakes in the valleys below. Visitors enjoy the High Peaks in any style, from casual hiking to serious rock climbing. Many start out their expeditions from Lake Placid.

Skiers discovered the slopes around this sparkling lake in the early twentieth century. Since then, the popular resort has hosted the Winter Olympic Games twice—in 1932 and 1980. Today, Olympic hopefuls train at Lake Placid's ski jumps, bobsled runs, and ice-skating rinks.

West of Lake Placid is a long chain of lakes—Lower, Middle, and Upper Saranac Lakes and Tupper Lake. The crisp air in this

Skiing is a favorite winter sport in the Adirondacks.

### Who Is Uncle Sam?

Uncle Sam—with his pointy white beard, red-and-white-striped top hat, and blue coat—is a familiar symbol of the U.S. government. He shows up in army posters and cartoons. But where did he come from?

The original Uncle Sam was Samuel Wilson, born in Massachusetts but a longtime resident of Troy, N.Y. During the War of 1812, he was a meatpacker who supplied beef to the army. Sam stamped U.S. BEEF on each shipment. Soldiers from his area knew that Sam was the packer, so they thought the stamp meant UNCLE SAM'S BEEF. Pretty soon, people were using UNCLE SAM to mean UNITED STATES.

Wilson is buried in Oakwood Cemetery, north of Troy. The local Boy Scouts raise the American flag over his grave every day. ■

region was once believed to be a cure for respiratory ailments. Robert Louis Stevenson came here for his health, and visitors can tour his cottage.

Lake George, in the park's southeast corner, is a popular spot for swimming, fishing, boating, and parasailing. The narrow La Chute River connects Lake George to Lake Champlain. The French built a fort there during the French and Indian Wars, but the British took it, renaming it Fort Ticonderoga. During the Revolutionary War, American patriots captured the fort. Fort Ticonderoga's museum traces its history, and costumed soldiers act out military maneuvers of the Revolutionary period.

## The Thousand Islands

The Thousand Islands region along the St. Lawrence River is shared by New York and Ontario, Canada. Cottages and mansions stand on most of the islands, though some islands are still untouched.

At the heart of the region is the resort community of Alexandria Bay. On nearby Heart Island is Boldt Castle, called the grandest of Gilded Age mansions. Multimillionaire George Boldt, owner of the Waldorf-Astoria Hotel, began building the ornate, 120-room castle

### Thousand Island Dressing

Thousand Island salad dressing came from the village of Clayton. Sophia LaLonde, wife of a Clayton fishing guide, concocted it in the early twentieth century. She gave the recipe to a local hotel owner, who began serving it to patrons in the restaurant. One day, millionaire George Boldt had a taste of the dressing. He liked it so much that he put it on the menu at the Waldorf-Astoria Hotel. Sophia's dressing has been famous ever since. ■

**Bridges connect the Thousand Islands region at many points.**

as a Valentine's Day gift for his wife, Louise. Tragically, she died before it was done.

Other towns in the area are Clayton and Cape Vincent, starting points for many fishing expeditions. Sackets Harbor was a great shipbuilding center during the War of 1812. In Ogdensburg is the Frederic Remington Art Museum, featuring his paintings and bronze sculptures on Wild West themes.

## Manhattan

Manhattan is the smallest of New York City's five boroughs and the center of the nation's finance, culture, publishing, and fashion. More than 1.5 million people live on the island.

It's easy to learn the layout of Manhattan. Its three main divisions are Downtown, Midtown, and Uptown. In Midtown and Uptown, streets are laid out in a regular grid. "Avenues" run north and south, and "streets" run east and west. The island's southern end is Downtown. Midtown is Manhattan's midsection. It runs from 14th Street up to the edge of Central Park at 59th Street. Uptown covers everything north of 59th Street.

## Midtown Manhattan

Broadway and Fifth Avenue are two of Manhattan's longest streets. Fifth Avenue is the dividing line between Manhattan's east and

**Manhattan is one of the world's most influential trade and financial centers.**

Times Square is in midtown Manhattan, where Broadway and Seventh Avenue meet.

## The Big Apple

New York City is called the Big Apple—but why? One story is that, when jazz musicians got a job in New York City, they used to say they were playing the Big Apple. A similar story says that the Big Apple was a jazz club in Harlem. Going to the Big Apple always meant going to New York City. ■

west sides, while Broadway cuts diagonally across much of Manhattan. On Fifth Avenue and 34th Street is the Empire State Building. *King Kong* and many other movies were filmed there. At 1,454 feet (443 m), it was the world's tallest building for forty years.

Fifth Avenue from 34th Street northward was once Manhattan's "Millionaires' Row." Wealthy tycoons, the cream of high society, built their mansions and brownstones there, and a few of them still stand.

Broadway and Seventh Avenue come together at Times Square, the heart of the theater district. This stretch of Broadway is so bright with theater lights and neon signs that it's called the Great White Way. Massive crowds turn out in Times Square for the big countdown on New Year's Eve, while millions watch the bash on TV.

On East 42nd Street is the landmark Grand Central Terminal Station. Its main concourse is a breathtaking space. Soaring above the high arched windows and chandeliers is a beautifully painted ceiling. Nearby is the Chrysler Building. It's a stunning art deco design, with layers of sun-ray arches at the top and red African marble in the lobby. To the east, along the waterfront, is the United Nations Headquarters. It spreads out over 18 acres (7.3 ha) along the East River.

Ice-skaters glide before the bronze statue of Prometheus, while flags of many nations flutter above. This is the wintertime scene in the plaza of Rockefeller Center. This massive entertainment and business complex covers about 25 acres (10 ha). Its tallest skyscraper is the G.E. Building. Luxurious Radio City Music Hall is

the largest indoor theater in the world. Nearby are the Museum of Modern Art and St. Patrick's Cathedral.

Rockefeller Center in winter

## Downtown Manhattan

Downtown is Manhattan's oldest section. Dutch settlers built a wall there for protection from the Indians. That's how Wall Street got its name. Off the tip of Manhattan stands Ellis Island, where millions of immigrants first landed, and the Statue of Liberty, symbolizing the freedom they sought. The Financial District centers on Wall and Broad Streets. In its tightly crowded skyscrapers are some of the world's most powerful banks, brokerages, and stock exchanges.

Near the New York Stock Exchange is Federal Hall, now a national memorial. From its balcony, George Washington took his oath of office as the first president. The hall was the nation's first capitol building. To the west, along the Hudson, are the 110-story twin towers of the World Trade Center. City hall and other government buildings cluster around the civic center.

To the north are some of Manhattan's oldest neighborhoods. Immigrants, especially Eastern European Jews, once settled in the Lower East Side and opened businesses there. Many still

**The New York Stock Exchange on Wall Street**

remain, though Puerto Ricans are its largest ethnic group now. Delicious aromas drift from the restaurants of Chinatown and Little Italy.

SoHo means "south of Houston" (pronounced HOW-ston) and TriBeCa stands for "Triangle Before Canal Street." Both are full of trendy art galleries and cafés. Greenwich Village has harbored artists, writers, and musicians since the nineteenth century.

## Uptown Manhattan

Central Park is Manhattan's most surprising feature. Surrounded with skyscrapers and tangled traffic, it covers 840 acres (340 ha) with grass, trees, and paths for strolling, jogging, biking, or horseback riding.

Fifth Avenue along Central Park's eastern edge is called Museum Mile. There stand the Frick Collection, the Metropolitan Museum of Art, the Solomon R. Guggenheim Museum, and the Museum of the City of New York. The Whitney Museum of Art is one block east on Madison Avenue. Along the eastern side of the

**Central Park offers New Yorkers an island of greenery amid the concrete jungle of city life.**

park is the Upper East Side. This area was once filled with slums. But after the Third Avenue elevated trains tracks were torn down in the early twentieth century, luxurious apartments and town houses were constructed for New York's wealthy.

Just north of Central Park is Harlem, a center of black culture and business enterprises. To the west of Harlem is Morningside Heights, home of Columbia University. In Washington Heights, at Manhattan's northern tip, is the Cloisters. This museum, a part of the Metropolitan Museum of Art, is devoted to the art of the Middle Ages.

## The Other Boroughs

The Bronx, northeast of Manhattan, was named for Jonas Bronck, a Swedish settler in the seventeenth century. In the center of the borough is Bronx Park, encompassing the Bronx Zoo and the New York Botanical Gardens. The zoo is the largest urban wildlife park in the country. Some of its several thousand inhabitants are giraffes, lions, Siberian tigers, Mongolian wild horses, and gorillas.

Staten Island is sometimes called the "forgotten borough." It's the least like the others in many ways. No bridge connects it to Manhattan—only a ferry.

The Staten Island Ferry runs frequently between Manhattan and Staten Island.

Today, visitors still enjoy the attractions of Coney Island.

It also escaped the heavy industrial buildup of the other boroughs. Staten Islanders voted to secede from New York City in 1993. They are waiting for the state legislature to approve the measure.

On much of Staten Island, the residential streets look like small-town neighborhoods in middle America. The borough's attractions include the Jacques Marchais Museum of Tibetan Art, Historic Richmond Town, and the cottage of early photographer Alice Austen.

Brooklyn sits on the southwestern tip of Long Island. It's connected to Manhattan across the East River via the Brooklyn, Manhattan, and Williamsburg Bridges. More people live in Brooklyn than in any of the other boroughs—almost 2.5 million people.

Downtown Brooklyn is clustered around the Brooklyn Bridge area. To the west and south is Brooklyn Heights, a very old neighborhood with beautiful brownstone homes. The Brooklyn Museum and the Brooklyn Academy of Music are major cultural sites. At the south end of Brooklyn is Coney Island. From the 1880s to the 1940s, it was a wildly popular resort and amusement park. Millions came to ride the roller coasters and the parachute jump or just stroll along the boardwalk eating hot dogs.

Queens is the largest borough in area and the second-largest in population. It lies east of Brooklyn on Long Island. Both La Guardia and John F. Kennedy Airports are in Queens. Homes cover most of the borough, while heavy industry is clustered along the East River. In the Queens Museum of Art is an enormous scale model of New York City, covering 9,000 square feet (836 sq m). The museum is in Flushing Meadows–Corona Park, site of New York's world's fairs of 1939–1940 and 1964–1965. Rockaway Beach and the Jamaica Bay Wildlife Refuge are on Queens's southern shore.

## Long Island

Long Island is about 120 miles (191 km) long. At its widest point, it measures only 23 miles (37 km). Elegant homes line the north shore, called the Gold Coast, while sandy beaches stretch for miles along the south. Long Island is one of the state's richest farming areas, too. Some parts of the island have a rural, country flavor.

Near Oyster Bay on the north shore is Sagamore Hill National Historic Site. It was Theodore Roosevelt's home and summer White House. Nearby is another famous estate, the Vanderbilt Mansion. Stony Brook recreates village life in the eighteenth century, with a blacksmith shop, schoolhouse, and other old buildings.

Whaling ships once sailed from Fire Island, off the south coast. Now most of the island is protected as Fire Island National Seashore. It's just one of Long Island's many oceanfront beaches. The Hamptons occupy a long stretch of the south shore. They are popular resorts and vacation communities.

**Docks at Greenport, Long Island**

# CHAPTER SEVEN

# Governing the Empire State

New York City as seen from Brooklyn

I t's a rule of thumb that's almost as old as the state itself: New York City is Democratic, while upstate New York is Republican. The rule still holds today.

In New York City, there are about five registered Democrats to every one registered Republican. The rest of the state typically votes for Republican candidates. The only exceptions are Albany and Erie Counties.

This actually makes for an even balance between Democrats and Republicans in the state as a whole. In the state legislature, Republicans usually dominate the senate, while Democrats are the majority in the assembly.

## The State Constitution

New York drew up its first state constitution in 1777—before it even *was* a state. The New York Colony was the first of the thirteen colonies to have its own constitution. It stated that, every twenty years, the voters could decide whether to hold another constitutional convention to change the document. New constitutions were adopted in 1821, 1846, and 1894.

Opposite: The downtown Government Center in Albany

## The State Symbols

**State bird: Bluebird** The bluebird (left) spends spring and summer in New York State. Its head, wings, and back are blue, and its breast is white, with an orange bib at the top. The bluebird population dropped to a low in the 1950s, but its numbers have risen again.

**State animal: Beaver** In the early seventeenth century, fur traders near present-day Albany traded with Indians for beaver skins. They shipped the furs back to Europe, where they were made into beaver hats and other clothing. Beavers grow to a length of 3 to 4 feet (1 to 1.2 m) and weigh 40 to 50 pounds (18 to 23 kg).

**State fish: Native brook trout** New York's brook trout are also called brookies or speckles. They live in lakes and ponds of the Adirondacks and in streams throughout the state.

**State tree: Sugar maple** A sweet sap oozes from the sugar maple in the spring. People collect it (below) to make maple syrup and sugar. Maple wood makes beautiful, sturdy furniture. It's also a good firewood for stoves and fireplaces. In the autumn, the sugar maple's leaves turn brilliant shades of red and orange.

**State flower: Rose** In 1891, New York schoolchildren were

asked to vote on their favorite flower. The rose came out at the top of the list. The state legislature made the rose—in all colors and varieties—the official state flower in 1955.

**State fruit: Apple** European settlers first brought apple seeds to New York in the 1600s. Colonists dried apples to eat during the winter. They also baked apple pies and fermented apples to make apple cider.

**State gem: Wine-red garnet** This dark red gem is used in jewelry and watch making and as an industrial abrasive. New York is the nation's top producer of garnets.

**State fossil: *Eurypterus remipes*** More than 400 million years ago, a shallow, salty sea covered central New York. Along the bottom crawled *Eurypterus remipes*. Now extinct, it was a relative of today's king crab and sea scorpion.

**State muffin: Apple muffin** Children at Bear Road Elementary School in North Syracuse were wild about apple muffins. They persuaded the governor to sign a bill declaring it the official state muffin. ■

## The State Flag

New York's state flag features the state coat of arms upon a dark blue field. The coat of arms features a shield with the goddesses Liberty and Justice on either side. Liberty stands with a crown at her feet. This symbolizes the American colonies' victory over the British monarchy in the Revolutionary War. Justice is blindfolded and holds the scales of justice. This means that all citizens are entitled to equal treatment under the law. In the center shield, ships of commerce sail the Hudson River as the sun rises over the Hudson Highlands. A banner at the bottom shows the state motto, EXCELSIOR, meaning "Ever Upward." ■

# New York's State Government

## Executive Branch

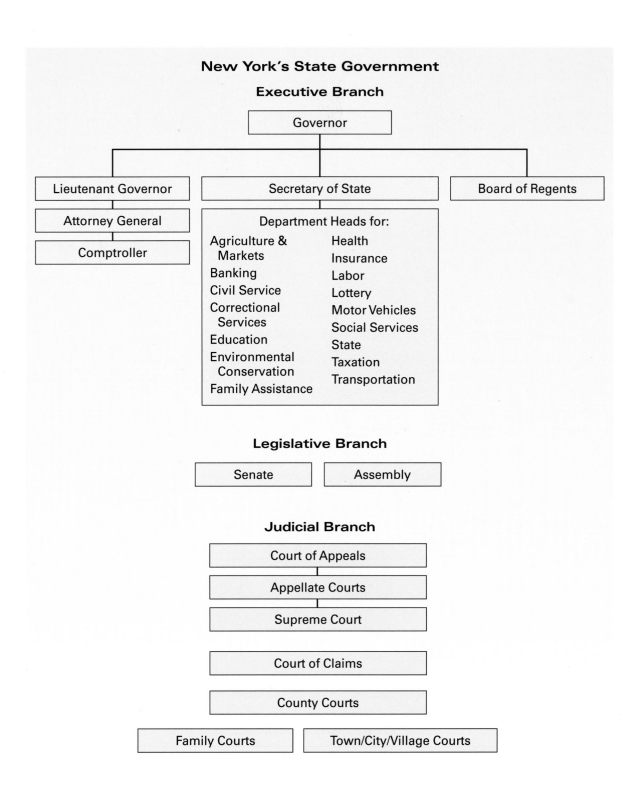

Governor

Lieutenant Governor

Secretary of State

Board of Regents

Attorney General

Comptroller

Department Heads for:

| | |
|---|---|
| Agriculture & Markets | Health |
| Banking | Insurance |
| Civil Service | Labor |
| Correctional Services | Lottery |
| Education | Motor Vehicles |
| Environmental Conservation | Social Services |
| Family Assistance | State |
| | Taxation |
| | Transportation |

## Legislative Branch

Senate

Assembly

## Judicial Branch

Court of Appeals

Appellate Courts

Supreme Court

Court of Claims

County Courts

Family Courts

Town/City/Village Courts

**The State Song**

**"I Love New York"**

Words and music by Steve Karmen

*I love New York,*
*I love New York,*
*I love New York.*
*There isn't another like it*
*No matter where you go.*
*And nobody can compare it.*
*It's win and place and show.*
*New York is special.*

*New York is diff'rent 'cause*
  *there's no place else on Earth*
  *quite like New York and that's*
  *why*
*I love New York,*
*I love New York,*
*I love New York.* ■

New York's constitution was also the first to provide that the governor be elected by the people. When New York was a colony, governors could appoint any state officials they pleased. Often these officials were wealthy friends who were not right for their jobs. The 1777 constitution tried to prevent this abuse. It made all appointments subject to the approval of a Council of Appointment made up of the governor and four senators.

The 1894 constitution remains in effect today. However, it has been amended, or changed, more than 200 times. Every twenty years, voters still have a chance to call for a constitutional convention. The legislature can make amendments to the constitution, too. Proposed amendments must be passed by two separately elected legislatures. Then the amendment goes before the voters in what's called a referendum. If it passes, it becomes part of the constitution.

## The Executive Branch

New York's governor is the head of the executive branch of state government. Voters elect the governor to a four-year term, and there

## New York's Governors

| Name | Party | Term | Name | Party | Term |
|------|-------|------|------|-------|------|
| George Clinton | None | 1777–1795 | Alonzo B. Cornell | Rep. | 1880–1882 |
| John Jay | Fed. | 1795–1801 | Grover Cleveland | Dem. | 1883–1885 |
| George Clinton | Dem.-Rep. | 1801–1804 | David Bennett Hill | Dem. | 1885–1891 |
| Morgan Lewis | Dem.-Rep. | 1804–1807 | Roswell Pettibone | | |
| Daniel D. Tompkins | Dem.-Rep. | 1807–1817 | Flower | Dem. | 1892–1894 |
| John Tayler | Dem.-Rep. | 1817 | Levi Parsons Morton | Rep. | 1895–1896 |
| De Witt Clinton | Dem.-Rep. | 1817–1822 | Frank Sweet Black | Rep. | 1897–1898 |
| Joseph C. Yates | Dem.-Rep. | 1823–1824 | Theodore Roosevelt | Rep. | 1899–1900 |
| De Witt Clinton | Dem.-Rep. | 1825–1828 | Benjamin B. Odell Jr. | Rep. | 1901–1904 |
| Nathaniel Pitcher | Ind. | 1828 | Frank Wayland Higgins | Rep. | 1905–1906 |
| Martin Van Buren | Dem.-Rep. | 1829 | Charles Evans Hughes | Rep. | 1907–1910 |
| Enos T. Throop | Dem. | 1829–1832 | Horace White | Rep. | 1910 |
| William L. Marcy | Dem. | 1833–1838 | John Alden Dix | Dem. | 1911–1912 |
| William H. Seward | Whig | 1839–1842 | William Sulzer | Dem. | 1913 |
| William C. Bouck | Dem. | 1843–1844 | Martin Henry Glynn | Dem. | 1913–1914 |
| Silas Wright | Dem. | 1845–1846 | Charles S. Whitman | Rep. | 1915–1918 |
| John Young | Whig | 1847–1848 | Alfred E. Smith | Dem. | 1919–1920 |
| Hamilton Fish | Whig | 1849–1850 | Nathan L. Miller | Rep. | 1921–1922 |
| Washington Hunt | Whig | 1851–1852 | Alfred E. Smith | Dem. | 1923–1928 |
| Horatio Seymour | Dem. | 1853–1854 | Franklin D. Roosevelt | Dem. | 1929–1932 |
| Myron Holley Clark | Whig | 1855–1856 | Herbert H. Lehman | Dem. | 1933–1942 |
| John Alsop King | Rep. | 1857–1858 | Charles Poletti | Dem. | 1942 |
| Edwin Denison Morgan | Rep. | 1859–1862 | Thomas E. Dewey | Rep. | 1943–1954 |
| Horatio Seymour | Dem. | 1863–1864 | W. Averell Harriman | Dem. | 1955–1958 |
| Reuben Eaton Fenton | Rep. | 1865–1868 | Nelson A. Rockefeller | Rep. | 1959–1973 |
| John Thompson | | | Malcolm Wilson | Rep. | 1973–1974 |
| Hoffman | Dem. | 1869–1872 | Hugh L. Carey | Dem. | 1975–1982 |
| John Adams Dix | Rep. | 1873–1874 | Mario M. Cuomo | Dem. | 1983–1994 |
| Samuel Jones Tilden | Dem. | 1875–1876 | George E. Pataki | Rep. | 1995– |
| Lucius Robinson | Dem. | 1877–1879 | | | |

### Mario Cuomo

Mario Cuomo was born in New York City in 1932 and attended St. John's University. He served as New York's governor from 1983 to 1994. Fellow Democrats urged Cuomo to seek the nomination for the U.S. presidency in 1984, 1988, and 1992. However, he declined. ■

is no limit on the number of terms a governor can serve. The lieutenant governor, attorney general, and comptroller are also elected to four-year terms.

The governor appoints many other officers in the executive branch. One is the secretary of state, but the legislature must approve this appointment. The governor also selects executive department heads that govern areas such as agriculture, transportation, and labor. One exception is the Board of Regents, which oversees education in the state. The legislature appoints these officials.

George E. Pataki

The New York State
capitol in Albany

### The Legislature

New York's legislature makes the state's laws. Like the U.S. Congress, the New York state legislature is composed of two houses: the state senate and the state assembly. This two-house legislature had its beginnings in the first state constitution of 1777. Voters from each district elect the 61 members of the Senate and 150 of the Assembly to two-year terms.

Legislators meet in the state capitol in Albany. They begin their regular legislative sessions on the first Wednesday after the first Monday in January. Sometimes a special session may be called to discuss an important issue.

Each house of the legislature has several committees. Members of a committee specialize in some area of public concern. When a bill, or proposed law, comes up, it goes to the proper committee first. Committee members discuss it and often change parts of it.

State legislators discussing business

## The Judicial System

New York's court system makes up the judicial branch of state government. Judges in the courts use state laws to decide whether someone has broken the law. In most other states, the supreme court is one group of judges that meets together in the state capital. In New York, however, supreme court judges are scattered throughout the state. Voters elect about 314 supreme court judges, and each judge serves a fourteen-year term.

Besides the supreme court judges, there are four sets of appellate judges. Appointed by the governor, they preside in the state's four judicial departments. When someone disagrees with a supreme court ruling, he or she may appeal the decision to an appellate court. The appellate court judges also hear appeals from lower state courts.

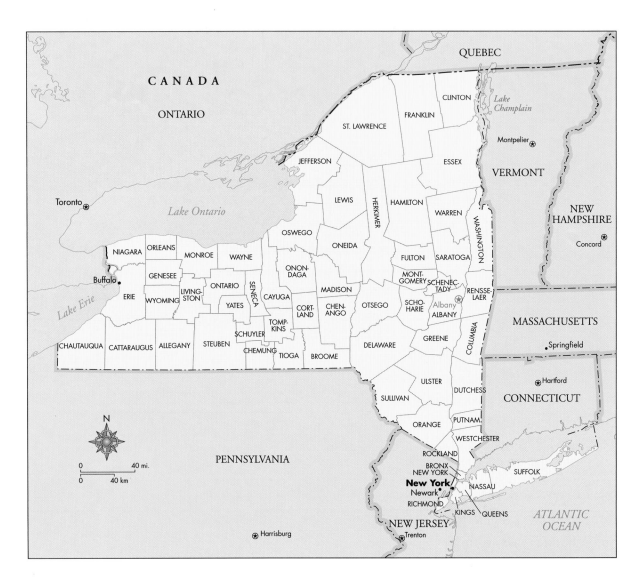

CANADA

ONTARIO

QUEBEC

Lake Champlain

CLINTON

FRANKLIN

ST. LAWRENCE

ESSEX

VERMONT

Montpelier

JEFFERSON

Toronto

Lake Ontario

LEWIS

HERKIMER

HAMILTON

WARREN

WASHINGTON

NEW HAMPSHIRE

Concord

NIAGARA

ORLEANS

MONROE

WAYNE

OSWEGO

ONEIDA

FULTON

SARATOGA

Buffalo

GENESEE

ONTARIO

SENECA

ONON-DAGA

MONT-GOMERY

SCHENEC-TADY

RENSSE-LAER

MASSACHUSETTS

Springfield

ERIE

WYOMING

LIVING-STON

YATES

CAYUGA

MADISON

SCHO-HARIE

Albany

ALBANY

Lake Erie

CORT-LAND

CHEN-ANGO

OTSEGO

COLUMBIA

TOMP-KINS

CHAUTAUQUA

CATTARAUGUS

ALLEGANY

STEUBEN

SCHUYLER

CHEMUNG

TIOGA

BROOME

DELAWARE

GREENE

Hartford

CONNECTICUT

ULSTER

DUTCHESS

SULLIVAN

N

ORANGE

PUTNAM

WESTCHESTER

PENNSYLVANIA

0    40 mi.
0    40 km

ROCKLAND

BRONX
NEW YORK

New York

Newark

NASSAU

SUFFOLK

ATLANTIC OCEAN

RICHMOND

KINGS

QUEENS

NEW JERSEY

Trenton

Harrisburg

**New York's counties**

New York's judicial system has another unusual twist. In most other states, the highest court is the state supreme court. But in New York, the highest court is the court of appeals. Its chief judge and six associate judges only hear appeals from the appellate courts. Judges in the court of appeals, like the appellate judges, are appointed by the governor. They are chosen from among the supreme court judges, and the state senate approves them.

Another New York court is the court of claims. It handles lawsuits against the state of New York. County courts hear civil and criminal cases that come up within each county. There are also family courts and town, city, and village courts.

## Local Government

New York is divided into sixty-two counties. Five of those counties are the boroughs of New York City: Staten Island is Richmond County; Manhattan is New York County; Brooklyn is Kings County; Bronx and Queens Counties share the name of their boroughs. A county board of supervisors typically governs a county. County governments are responsible for parks, libraries, county courts, welfare, and highways.

Within each county are cities, towns, and villages. Cities and towns are usually governed by a mayor and council or a supervisor and board of supervisors. Villages elect mayors, too. But a village remains part of a larger city or town. That means that village residents often have to pay both village taxes and city taxes.

More than half of New York's state budget goes to the local governments. Local officials spend most of this money on public schools. Other funds go to highways, public housing, and welfare.

# CHAPTER EIGHT

# Making a Living

N ew York produces more goods and services than many entire nations do. If New York State were a country, it would have one of the top fifteen economies in the world.

## Manufacturing

New York's manufacturing output is second only to California's. In fact, the value of New York's manufactured goods makes up 7 percent of the nation's entire production.

Assembling Xerox copiers in a Rochester factory

Manufacturing accounts for over one-eighth of New York's gross state product, or GSP. (The GSP is the total value of all goods and services the state produces in a year.) About a million New Yorkers work in the state's 30,000 factories.

New York leads the nation in printing and publishing. Books, magazines, newspapers, and other printed materials are New York's leading factory goods. One-sixth of all the printing and publishing in the country takes place in New York City. It's the world headquarters for magazines such as *Time* and *Newsweek*; newspapers such as *The Wall Street Journal, The New York Times*, and *USA Today*; and book publishers such as Bantam Doubleday Dell, Macmillan, and Random House.

The Rochester area is one of the top manufacturing spots in the country. Its factories make cameras, film, copy machines, and

Opposite: Stock market traders on Wall Street

Making a Living **91**

instruments for dentists and eye doctors. Rochester is also the home of the Eastman Kodak Company.

Factories in Buffalo make medical and surgical equipment and electrical machinery. New York City factories make clocks, watches, and many types of medical and engineering instruments. Chemicals, electronic parts, and electrical equipment and machinery are some of the state's other manufactured goods. Many residents in the cities of Poughkeepsie, Schenectady, Binghamton, Syracuse, and Utica are factory workers.

## The Clothing Scene

Calvin Klein and Donna Karan are just two of New York City's world-class fashion designers. But high fashion is only a part of the city's clothing scene. New York City is the country's leading manufacturer of women's clothes.

The city's garment industry grew up in the nineteenth century, when thousands of new immigrants found jobs in clothing workshops. In its early days, the garment industry was centered in Manhattan's Lower East Side. Now, much of the labor takes place in Chinatown, Brooklyn's Sunset Park, and Flushing in Queens. Even today, immigrants are likely to find their first jobs in New York City's garment trade.

## Farming for the Masses

Manhattanites think they work hard. But across upstate New York, long before the sun is up, dairy farmers are already on the job. They're in the milking barn, hooking cows up to mechanized pumps for their morning milking. Each cow will give about 2 gallons (7.6 l) of milk then and another 2 gallons in the afternoon milking. At 4 gallons a day, New York's total cow population produces more than 20 million gallons (76 million l) of milk every week!

New York is one of the top dairy states in the nation. Dairy products account for over half of the state's total farm income. More than 10,000 dairy farms operate in the state, and most of them are in the north. An average New York dairy farmer owns about seventy cows. In Lewis County, there are more cows than there are people!

New York farmers also raise beef cattle, hogs, pigs, sheep, chickens, turkeys, and ducks. Hog and sheep farms are com-

**A dairy farm in Amsterdam**

Vineyards along Seneca Lake in the Finger Lakes region

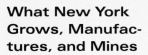

**What New York Grows, Manufactures, and Mines**

**Agriculture**

Milk
Apples
Hay
Corn

**Manufacturing**

Printed materials
Scientific instruments
Machinery
Chemicals

**Mining**

Crushed stone ■

mon in the western part of the state. More than half the farm-raised ducks in the country come from Suffolk County on Long Island. Suffolk County is a top chicken-and-egg region, too. So is Sullivan County in the Catskills.

Crops bring in about one-third of New York's farm income. The most important crops are hay, corn, and alfalfa for animal feed. Cabbage, potatoes, sweet corn, and snap beans are some of the major field crops. Farms on Long Island provide New York City's homes and restaurants with a good supply of fresh vegetables.

Apples are New York's major fruit. They grow in many of the state's 3,000 orchards. Some of the biggest apple orchards lie along Lake Ontario and the Hudson River. Cherries are another common orchard fruit. Some fruit farmers let people come and pick the fruit themselves.

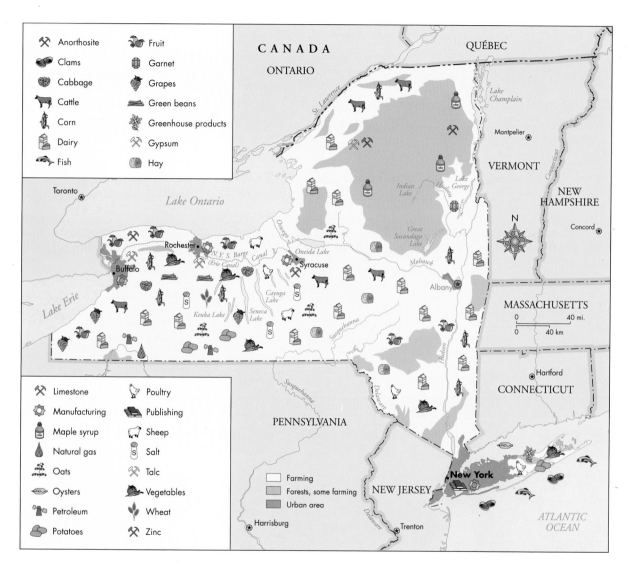

**Map legend:**

| Symbol | Label | Symbol | Label |
|---|---|---|---|
| | Anorthosite | | Fruit |
| | Clams | | Garnet |
| | Cabbage | | Grapes |
| | Cattle | | Green beans |
| | Corn | | Greenhouse products |
| | Dairy | | Gypsum |
| | Fish | | Hay |

| Symbol | Label | Symbol | Label |
|---|---|---|---|
| | Limestone | | Poultry |
| | Manufacturing | | Publishing |
| | Maple syrup | | Sheep |
| | Natural gas | | Salt |
| | Oats | | Talc |
| | Oysters | | Vegetables |
| | Petroleum | | Wheat |
| | Potatoes | | Zinc |

Farming
Forests, some farming
Urban area

**New York's natural resources**

New York's grapes make fine wines. Chautauqua County, New York's westernmost county, is the state's major grape producer. New Yorkers also grow greenhouse and nursery items such as flowers, bulbs, and seeds. Here, too, Long Island's Suffolk County is the top producer.

## Mining and Minerals

When you strike a match and watch it burn, what makes the flame burn evenly? It's a New York mineral called woolastonite. The country's only major woolastonite mine is located in New York State. Woolastonite is part of our everyday lives, but not many people are aware of it. Its brilliant white color makes it a great tooth cleaner. And because it's so tough, it's also used in making car bumpers.

What do the Adirondacks and the moon have in common? They're two of the best places to find anorthosite. This durable rock is common in the mountains of the moon. But it occurs in only a few spots on the face of the Earth. New York's Mount Marcy and Whiteface Mountain are composed mainly of anorthosite. The rock was used in paving Albany's Empire State Plaza.

**Mining rock salt in Lansing**

Garnet, the state gem, is best known for its use in jewelry. However, when crushed and ground, garnet becomes a scratchy surface for sandpaper. Garnets are also put into watches to help them run smoothly. One of the world's largest garnet mines is located near North Creek in Warren County.

Stone, portland cement, salt, and sand and gravel are New York's leading minerals.

The state's major stone is limestone. Most of the limestone is crushed to make surfaces for roads. Salt wells abound in western New York's Appalachian region. They produce both table salt and the salt used to melt ice on sidewalks and roads. Among New York's metals, zinc is the most valuable. New York is one of the top four states to yield garnets, zinc, talc, and salt.

## Repairing the Land

Mining operations sometimes tear up many acres of forestland and wildlife habitats. By state law, mining and drilling companies have to repair their damage to the environment. Some companies go far beyond what the law requires.

The Galster Sand and Gravel Pit in Onondaga County once covered 36 acres (15 ha) at a depth of 20 feet (6 m). The mine owner turned the site into a 20-acre (8-ha) lake surrounded by recreation, sports, and picnic areas. Foxes, deer, geese, and blue herons now make their homes in the area, too.

## Communication

"All the News That's Fit to Print" —that's the famous motto of *The New York Times*. The *Times* enjoys a worldwide reputation for serious journalism on politics, economics, science, and culture.

New York publishes more magazines, newspapers, and books than any other state. New York's publishing industry began in 1725 with its first newspaper, the *New York Gazette.* Today, New York publishes hundreds of newspapers. More than eighty are daily papers.

Businesspeople all over the world read *The Wall Street Journal.* Other important papers are the *New York Post* and the New York

## Freedom of the Press

New York's first newspaper, the *New York Gazette,* was a mouthpiece for the British colonial government. But German immigrant John Peter Zenger wanted readers to hear another point of view. He started a rival newspaper, the *New York Weekly Journal*, in 1733. Its articles viciously attacked the corrupt colonial governor, William Cosby. Cosby had Zenger jailed and put on trial for criminal libel. (Libel is the publication of lies about someone.)

Philadelphia lawyer Andrew Hamilton rushed to Zenger's rescue. In a brilliant defense, he argued that Zenger couldn't be guilty because the things he published were true, not false. The jury found Zenger innocent. This helped to establish the principle of freedom of the press, which became a cornerstone of the U.S. Constitution. Today, the John Peter Zenger Memorial Room is part of Manhattan's Federal Hall Memorial Museum. ■

*Daily News.* They focus on human-interest stories rather than on national and international news. Dozens of ethnic groups in New York publish foreign-language newspapers, too.

New York's first radio station was WGY. It began broadcasting from Schenectady in 1922. Four years later, the National Broadcasting Company (NBC) started the nation's first coast-to-coast radio network. In 1941, NBC established the first commercial television station in the country. New York City is now the head-

## Joseph Pulitzer

Joseph Pulitzer (1847–1911) was a newspaper editor and publisher. Born in Hungary, he came to the United States in 1864. While working as a newspaper reporter in St. Louis, Missouri, he was elected to the Missouri legislature. Then he began buying small newspaper companies.

His purchase of the *New York World* in 1883 made him wealthy. In 1903, Pulitzer announced that he would donate money to open Columbia University's School of Journalism.

He left his fortune to provide the famous Pulitzer Prizes. They are awarded every year for outstanding work in literature, drama, history, music, and journalism. ■

quarters for the three major TV networks—NBC (National Broadcasting Company), CBS (Columbia Broadcasting System), and ABC (American Broadcasting Company).

## Getting There and Getting Around

New York's early residents were good at finding ways to travel long distances. The Hudson–Mohawk Valley was the best way to get through the Appalachian Mountains to the Great Lakes. The Erie Canal made the trip even faster and smoother.

Today, the New York State Barge Canal System is one of the longest inland waterways in the country. It follows the Erie Canal's route and adds a northern leg from the Hudson up to Lake Champlain. From one end to the other, it covers about 800 miles (1,287 km). The canal system is still the shortest water route from the Atlantic Ocean to the Great Lakes. Since the 1950s, the canal has transported fewer cargo ships and more pleasure boats. But for bulky cargo such as petroleum products, the canal is still the best way to travel.

New York's highways run along many of the same routes that the old turnpikes took. They're just wider, straighter, and better paved. The Thomas E. Dewey Thruway (Interstate 87) is the longest toll superhighway in the world. It runs all the way from New York City to the state's northern border with Quebec. Interstate highways give travelers easy access to Canada, as well as to neighboring states. In central New York, Interstate 81 runs north and south from Pennsylvania through Binghamton to the Canadian border. It intersects with the Dewey Thruway at Syracuse.

New York's first railroad, the Mohawk and Hudson, opened in

**Rush-hour traffic on Fifth Avenue**

1831. It followed the Mohawk from Albany to Schenectady. But Cornelius Vanderbilt's New York Central Railroad became the largest train system in the state. It connected New Yorkers with Chicago, Boston, Montreal (Canada), and other big cities. Today, New York's railroads carry more freight than people. They transport much of the ship cargo that arrives in New York Harbor—one of the largest seaports in the world.

John F. Kennedy International Airport and La Guardia Airport are New York's major airports. But many travelers prefer to get to and from New York City through Newark Airport in nearby New Jersey. The Port Authority of New York and New Jersey operates New York's shipping ports and airports.

## Getting Around in the Big Apple

A Manhattan resident doesn't really need a car. Besides, driving is nerve-wracking, traffic often jams to a dead halt, and there's nowhere to park. It's much easier to leave driving to the experts—those fearless cabbies who navigate the "sea of yellow."

Transportation played a big part in New York City's growth. When Cornelius Vander-

bilt built Grand Central Termi-
anl as the endpoint of his railroad, it made Midtown
Manhattan an important business district. Pennsylvania Station, beneath Madison Square
Garden, is Manhattan's other
major train station.

The Brooklyn Bridge, com-
pleted in 1883, made it easier
for Manhattan's teeming population to spill over into Brooklyn. At the time, it was the
longest bridge in the world. It's
now a national historic landmark. The Verrazano-Narrows
Bridge, built in 1964 between

The Brooklyn Bridge,
looking toward Man-
hattan

Brooklyn and Staten Island, is one of the longest suspension
bridges in the world. Several other bridges span the Hudson and the
East Rivers. The Holland and Lincoln Tunnels run under the Hudson between New York and New Jersey. The Queens Midtown
Tunnel connects Queens and Manhattan. And the Battery Tunnel
connects Manhattan to Brooklyn.

Manhattan's subway system opened in 1904. Over the years, it
expanded to reach the other boroughs. Thanks to the subways,
people quickly built homes in Brooklyn, the Bronx, and Queens. It
was easy to take the subway to their jobs in Manhattan. Now New
York City has an extensive subway and bus system.

# CHAPTER NINE

# Faces in the Crowd

alking along the streets of Manhattan is the best way to experience New York's human flavor. Ethnic restaurants and markets, foreign-language newspapers, and faces and fashions from every corner of the Earth make the city a vibrant, exciting community.

The state's ethnic diversity began in the seventeenth century with the New Amsterdam colony. Dutch settlers founded the colony. But by the time its population reached 1,000, residents spoke more than fifteen different languages.

Today, New Yorkers claim ancestors from practically every country on Earth. In the 1990 census, the most commonly reported ancestries and ethnic origins were African, Hispanic, Italian, German, Irish, English, Polish, Russian, French, Dutch, Scottish, Greek, Hungarian, and French Canadian.

A country fair in
upstate New York

## A Refuge for All

Each group had its own special reasons for migrating. For many, the United States meant religious freedom. New York's first religious refugees were French Huguenots. They populated New York's first white settlement at present-day Albany. Religious persecution in the eighteenth century brought in a wave of Germans. Many settled near Newburgh in the Hudson Valley and around Schoharie in

Opposite: Crowds on
Fifth Avenue

**A Puerto Rican Day parade**

the Mohawk Valley. Pogroms, or bloody massacres, across Eastern Europe later sent hundreds of thousands of Jewish people to American shores.

Other immigrants simply hoped to make a living. A potato famine in Ireland sent thousands of Irish people to New York in the mid-nineteenth century. Earlier Irish immigrants laborers helped build the Erie Canal and the state's first railroads.

In the early twentieth century, Italian immigrants settled in central New York. Many worked in the knitting mills of Utica and the copper mills of Rome. The industrial towns of Buffalo, Syracuse, and Schenectady saw an influx of Polish, Lithuanian, Romanian, and Russian people. Around the same time, Binghamton claimed to have twenty-six ethnic groups among its factory workers.

## Speaking in Many Tongues

Even today, about 16 percent of all New Yorkers were born outside the United States. Although most immigrants and their children learn English, hundreds of thousands of New Yorkers still speak another language when they're at home. Often, the native language survives even after a family has been in the United States for many generations.

The most widely spoken "home languages" in New York are Spanish, Italian, Chinese, French, German, Polish, and Yiddish. Yiddish is a form of German mixed with Hebrew. It is spoken by many Jewish people of East European origin.

## No Longer the Biggest

The 1990 census counted about 18 million people in New York State. That made New York the second most populous state in the country. Only California had more residents. But in the census bureau's estimates for 1997, New York had dropped to third place—falling behind both California and Texas.

This is quite a change for the Empire State. From 1820 through 1960, New York's population ranked number one in the nation. But California pulled ahead to first place in the 1970 census.

## Lopsided Living Spaces

If New Yorkers were spread out evenly across the state, there would be about 367 people on every square mile (142 per sq km). If the state were divided into football fields, that would give about one and a half football fields to every man, woman, and child.

But in reality, New York's population is spread out quite *un*-evenly. Only about one-sixth of New Yorkers live in rural areas, while the rest live in or near cities or towns. The "emptiest" part of the state is the rugged Adirondack region of northern New York.

In contrast, more than 40 percent of the state's entire population lives in New York City. On Manhattan, people are tightly packed. About 69,040 people live on every square mile (26,656 per sq km) of the island. How tight is that? It's as crowded as if

**Population of New York's Major Cities (1990)**

| | |
|---|---|
| New York City | 7,322,564 |
| Buffalo | 328,123 |
| Rochester | 231,636 |
| Yonkers | 188,082 |
| Syracuse | 163,860 |
| Albany | 101,082 |

**Commuters waiting for a train**

every 120 Manhattanites made their homes on one football field!

## Cities

New York City is not only the largest city in the state. It's also the largest city in the country. A total of about 7.3 million people live in its five boroughs of Manhattan, Brooklyn, the Bronx, Queens, and Staten Island. Manhattan alone is home to about 1.5 million people.

New York City's metropolitan area covers a broad area. It includes not only part of New York, but also nearby counties in New Jersey and Connecticut. More than 8.5 million people live in this metropolitan area. The country's only urban area with a higher population is Los Angeles, California.

Buffalo, in the far west, is the state's second-largest city, with about 328,000 residents. The north-central city of Rochester ranks third, with about 232,000. Yonkers and Syracuse are the next largest. Albany, the capital, is the state's sixth-largest city.

## The City versus the State

If we look at the human makeup of New York City and upstate New York, they almost seem like two different states. Only about 10 percent of upstaters belong to nonwhite ethnic groups. But in New York City, almost half the residents are nonwhite.

About 16 percent of all New Yorkers are African-Americans. But in New York City, the figure is 25 percent. After World War I,

## Buffalo Wings

This dish, invented in Buffalo, New York, has become a favorite around the country.

**Ingredients:**
- 4 lbs. chicken wings
- salt and pepper
- 4 cups vegetable oil
- 1/2 stick butter
- 1 tbsp. white vinegar
- 1/4 cup Anchor Bar Sauce, Frank's Red Hot sauce, or hot sauce of your choice
- celery, sliced lengthwise
- blue cheese dressing

**Directions:**

Chop each chicken wing in half and remove the tip. Season with salt and pepper.

Heat the oil in a deep skillet until it starts to pop. Add half the wings and cook, stirring occasionally, for 10–15 minutes—until they turn a golden brown.

Drain on paper towels, then place wings in a bowl.

Preheat oven to 350°F.

Melt the butter in a heavy saucepan then add the vinegar and hot sauce. Remove from heat and stir well. Pour the sauce over the wings and stir carefully, making sure to coat each wing in the sauce. Place the wings on a cookie sheet and pour any remaining sauce over the top.

Bake for 5 to 10 minutes until the coating becomes crispy.

Serve with sliced celery and blue cheese dressing.

Serves 8.

most newcomers to New York City were blacks from the South. They hoped to find better jobs and to escape racist groups such as the Ku Klux Klan. Many settled in Harlem. Today, Bedford-Stuyvesant in Brooklyn is New York City's largest African-American neighborhood.

**Shopping in Chinatown**

People of Hispanic origin make up 24 percent of New York City's population. But in the state as a whole, only 12 percent are Hispanic. About half of the state's Hispanics are Puerto Ricans. Others originate from the Dominican Republic, Colombia and other South American countries, Mexico, Cuba, and Central American countries such as El Salvador, Panama, Honduras, and Guatemala.

Most of New York's Asian people live in New York City. They represent about 7 percent of the city's population. Chinese people are the largest Asian group. Others include Koreans, East Indians, Pakistanis, Japanese, Thai, and Vietnamese.

## Native Americans

The whole state of New York was once Native American land. Today, Indian reservations occupy only about 0.4 percent of that land. The 1990 census counted about 61,000 Native Americans in New York State.

Descendents of the six nations of the Iroquois Confederacy still make their homes in the state. The Iroquois once envisioned their

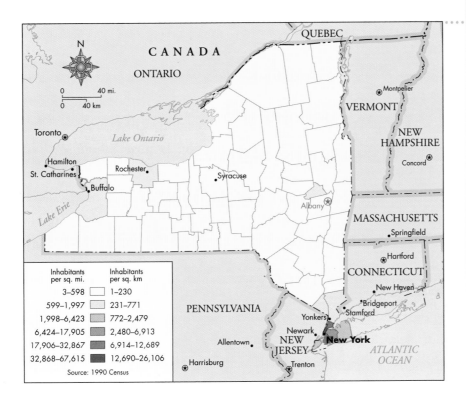

Descendants of the Iroquois Confederacy celebrating their traditions on the Onondaga Nation reservation near Syracuse

league as a great longhouse stretching across what is now New York. The Seneca, at the western end, were known as the Keepers of the Western Door. Today, the Seneca Nation is the largest group among the Iroquois. Three Seneca reservations are located in western New York. The Tonawanda band of Senecas has its own reservation.

The St. Regis Mohawk tribe is the second-largest Iroquois group. Mohawk territory in far-northern New York extends into Ontario. Mohawks have distinguished themselves as expert high-altitude ironworkers. They helped build many of New York City's bridges and skyscrapers.

The Oneida call themselves the People of the Standing Stone. The Oneida Nation of central New York is the largest employer in

Above left: New York's population density map

Madison and Oneida Counties. Oneida enterprises include a grand resort hotel, a casino, campgrounds, retail stores, and a textile factory.

The Onondaga Nation's reservation is near Syracuse. The Onondagan named Ayawentha (Hiawatha) is remembered for helping to bring about the Iroquois's great peace accord. The Tuscarora joined the Iroquois in the eighteenth century after being driven out of North Carolina. Their reservation is north of Buffalo. The Cayuga, the smallest group, has no reservation. Most members live near the Senecas' Allegany Reservation.

Two non-Iroquois groups live on Long Island. They occupy the Shinnecock and Poospatuck reservations.

## Education

New York's first schools opened in New Amsterdam in the seventeenth century. They were set up by churches and received government support, too. Today, the state still provides some funds to private schools. Many New Yorkers want to change the state constitution so that only public schools are state supported.

New York's first public school opened in 1791. A statewide system of public elementary schools was in place by 1812. Parents paid part of their children's tuition until 1867, when public schools were finally free. Now all children in New York are required to attend school from age six through age six-

**A fifth-grade class in a public school**

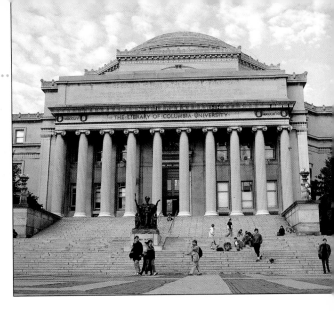

**Columbia University**

teen. (Buffalo and New York City require attendance through age seventeen.)

New York's legislature set up the Board of Regents in 1784. Its role today is the same as it was then. The board oversees schools throughout the state—more than 5,000 schools in all. That includes both public and private schools, from prekindergarten through universities. The sixteen-member Board of Regents sets the educational standards for each level, approves the opening of new schools, and distributes state school funds.

Public colleges and universities are part of the State University of New York (SUNY), established in 1948. This system comprises more than seventy schools, including two-year community colleges. Both state and city funds support the City University of New York (CUNY) system.

New York's largest private college is New York University, with more than 30,000 students. The oldest is Columbia University. It began in 1754 as King's College. Catholic universities include Fordham in the Bronx and St. John's in Jamaica, Queens. New York City's Union Theological Seminary and Yeshiva University are prominent schools for religious instruction.

The Juilliard School, the University of Rochester, and the Manhattan School of Music are renowned music schools. The Cooper Union specializes in architecture, engineering, and art. Cornell University, Syracuse University, Union University, Vassar College, Colgate University, and Skidmore College are some of New York's many other fine colleges and universities.

# CHAPTER TEN

# Culture and Fun

**An outdoor café in Manhattan's Greenwich Village**

**W**here did Rip Van Winkle take his twenty-year nap? In a ravine high in the Catskill Mountains. At least, that's where Washington Irving placed him. There are still some old-timers who swear they can point out the very spot where Rip slept. They even know the dent in the rock where Rip's shoulder lay.

Irving is best known for "Rip Van Winkle" (1819) and "The Legend of Sleepy Hollow" (1820). Rip, the spooky Headless Horseman, and gawky Ichabod Crane are some of Irving's most unforgettable characters. He based many of his tales on old Dutch legends of the Hudson Valley. When Irving made fun of New York's wealthy Dutch residents, he used the pen name Diedrich Knickerbocker. And it was Irving who gave New York City the nickname Gotham.

James Fenimore Cooper lived much of his life in Cooperstown, a town his father founded. He is best known for his frontier tales—*The Last of the Mohicans, The Deerslayer, The Pathfinder,* and others in the Leatherstocking Tales. They tell episodes in the life of frontiersman Natty Bumppo, also known as Hawkeye, and his Indian companion, Chingachgook.

Walt Whitman is often called the country's greatest poet. Born on Long Island in 1819, Whitman was the editor of the *Brooklyn Eagle.* Later he published his famous book of poetry, *Leaves of Grass* (1855). New Yorker Herman Melville, born the same year as Whitman, wrote the great sea adventure *Moby-Dick.*

**Opposite: Sunnyside, the country home of Washington Irving**

## The Invention of Santa Claus

To the Dutchmen of New York, St. Nicholas was a serious-faced holiday visitor dressed in dark clothes. But New Yorker Clement Clarke Moore changed that image forever. On Christmas Eve 1822, he sat down and wrote a poem for his children called "A Visit from St. Nicholas." We know it now as "The Night before Christmas."

Moore told of a jolly-faced, twinkly-eyed St. Nick—said to be modeled after Moore's Dutch caretaker. The reindeer names were inspired by Gnasher and Cracker—mythical goats who pulled the chariot of Thor, the German god of thunder. Moore's poem was an instant success. Cartoonist Thomas Nast added more details to the jolly fellow—the red, fur-trimmed suit; the long, curved pipe; and the bulging bag of gifts. A serious scholar and professor, Moore was too embarrassed to admit he wrote the poem until 1844. ■

Edgar Allan Poe lived in the Bronx and in Greenwich Village. There he wrote many of his spine-tingling tales. His poem "The Raven" first appeared in the *New York Evening Mirror* in 1845.

In the early twentieth century, Manhattan's Greenwich Village became a haven for artists and writers. Marianne Moore and Edna St. Vincent Millay wrote poetry there. Theodore Dreiser and Thomas Wolfe wrote novels, and Eugene O'Neill wrote plays.

Edith Wharton told stories about both the downtrodden and the wealthy people of her hometown, New York City. Her novel *The Age of Innocence* (1920) won the Pulitzer Prize.

Lovers of fine literature founded *The New Yorker* magazine in 1925. It has published stories by many of the country's finest writers. Some famous contributors have been novelists John Updike and Saul Bellow and humorist James Thurber.

In the 1920s, African-Americans in Manhattan's Harlem district began a literary movement called the Harlem Renaissance. One outspoken figure in this period was James Weldon Johnson. His *Book of American Negro Poetry* (1922) was the country's first major collection of poems by African-Americans. Other notable works of this movement were poetry by Langston Hughes and Countee Cullen and novels by Claude McKay and Zora Neale Hurston.

After World War II, New York City quickly became the center of the literary world. Neil Simon turned out comic plays such as *Barefoot in the Park, The Odd Couple,* and *The Heartbreak Kid.* Arthur Miller won the Pulitzer Prize for his tragic play *Death of a Salesman.* New York's countless other literary figures include novelists E. L. Doctorow *(Ragtime* and *Billy Bathgate)* and Tom Wolfe *(Bonfire of the Vanities).*

## The Great White Way

To perform on Broadway is the dream of millions of young actors, singers, and dancers. Most of the country's blockbuster plays and

**A Broadway theater**

musicals start out on Broadway. From there, they go on tour around the country—maybe even for years. The most popular shows of all keep playing on Broadway, packing in crowds every night.

Broadway was an exciting place in the 1920s and 1930s. Irving Berlin, Jerome Kern, and George and Ira Gershwin were writing musicals that, it seems, will never die. Today the Gershwins' *Porgy and Bess* and Kern's *Showboat* are more popular than ever.

Broadway shows aren't necessarily located on Broadway itself. The term refers to

**Carnegie Hall**

**The Metropolitan Opera House at Lincoln Center for the Performing Arts**

any show presented in Manhattan's theater district. It runs from 40th to 57th Streets, between Eighth Avenue and the Avenue of the Americas. The heart of the district is Times Square, where Broadway and Seventh Avenue come together at a sharp angle. With its bright lights and bigger-than-life electric billboards, this is truly the Great White Way.

## The Classical Music Scene

For musicians, playing in New York's Carnegie Hall means they've reached the peak of their profession. Built in 1891, Carnegie Hall has hosted the greatest musicians in the world—from Russian composer and conductor Pyotr Ilich Tchaikovsky to the Beatles in 1964. For opera singers, appearing with "the Met" is a landmark event. The Met, or Metropolitan Opera, is just but one tenant of the massive Lincoln Center for the Performing Arts.

Lincoln Center covers 16 acres (6.5 ha) of Manhattan's Upper West Side. Within the arts complex are the Metropolitan Opera House, Avery Fisher Hall, the New York State Theater, the Juilliard School of Music, the New York Public Library for the Performing Arts, and Alice Tully Hall. Lincoln Center also includes a bandshell and outdoor plazas for free summer concerts.

## George Gershwin

Composer George Gershwin (1898–1937) was born in Brooklyn. The son of Russian Jewish immigrants, he was originally named Jacob Gershvin. He began playing the piano as a child. At age fifteen, he left school and went to work in Tin Pan Alley, where pianists played the tunes of songwriters who hoped to get published. Gershwin wrote his own first hit, "Swanee," in 1919. He went on to write an astonishing number of songs and musicals, with his brother Ira writing the lyrics for many of them. Gershwin left behind some of the world's most popular songs—including "I Got Rhythm" and "Someone to Watch over Me"—as well as the jazz concert piece *Rhapsody in Blue* and the folk opera *Porgy and Bess.* ◾

Avery Fisher Hall is the home of the New York Philharmonic, the oldest symphony orchestra in the country. Juilliard is one of the top arts schools in the world. It trains not only musicians but also actors and dancers.

When they're not on the road, both the American Ballet Theater and the New York City Ballet perform in Lincoln Center. The Alvin Ailey Dance Company, the Dance Theater of Harlem, and the Martha Graham Dance Company are some other New York troupes that tour widely.

Music and dance thrive outside of New York City, too. The Eastman School of Music in Rochester is known worldwide for its high-quality students, teachers, and concerts. Rochester, Buffalo, and many other cities have their own symphony orchestras. People who live in college towns enjoy a variety of concerts at their hometown schools.

In the summer, Saratoga Springs is alive with music and dance. The city's Saratoga Performing Arts Center is the summer home of the Philadelphia Symphony Orchestra, the New York City Ballet, and the New York City Opera. The center also hosts jazz concerts and theater performances.

## George Balanchine

George Balanchine (1904–1983) was one of the world's finest choreographers. Born in St. Petersburg, Russia, he was originally named Georgy Balanchivadze. He trained at the School of Imperial Ballet and, while on a European tour in 1924, defected to the West. In 1933, Balanchine moved to New York. He became the choreographer for the New York City Ballet when it was founded in 1948. Balanchine created dances for movies and Broadway plays, as well as for pieces by Igor Stravinsky and other great composers. His holiday classic, *The Nutcracker*, with music by Tchaikovsky, remains a popular favorite today. ■

## Art

Gorgeous scenery in the Hudson River valley inspired many artists of the 1800s. Thomas Cole, Frederic E. Church, Albert Bierstadt, and others painted shimmering landscapes set in the valley and in the Catskill Mountains. Their style, called the Hudson River school, was the first truly American style of painting. Before this time, most artists in the United States copied European art styles.

New York City gave the nation its first big dose of modern art in 1913. The International Exhibition of Modern Art showed hundreds of works by Europeans who were experimenting with modern styles such as cubism and postimpressionism. The show inspired wealthy art lovers to donate huge sums to the arts. Their donations established New York City's Museum of Modern Art (1929), the Whitney Museum of American Art (1931), and the Guggenheim Foundation (1937). Today, the Museum of Modern Art (MOMA) is one of the world's top museums.

**Along the Hudson, by John Frederick, 1852**

## The Metropolitan Museum of Art

The Metropolitan Museum of Art opened in 1872. Located on Manhattan's Fifth Avenue, it's the largest museum in the Western Hemisphere. Its collections grew as wealthy New Yorkers donated money and their family art treasures. Today, the Met covers about 2 million square feet (185,806 sq m) and houses almost 3 million pieces of art, sculpture, and other precious objects. Only about one-fourth of them can be shown at once. ■

Andy Warhol's famous painting of Marilyn Monroe

In the 1930s, many of Europe's modern artists moved to New York City. By the time World War II was over, American artists had developed their own modern style. Abstract expressionism, also called the New York school, featured wild brush strokes, dripped and splattered paint drops, and solid color fields. In the 1950s, some of the leading abstract expressionists were Willem de Kooning, Jackson Pollock, and Mark Rothko.

Pop art was born in the 1960s, and New York artists paved the way. The leaders were Andy Warhol, Robert Rauschenberg, Claes Oldenburg, and Roy Lichtenstein. Warhol's Campbell's soup cans and Marilyn Monroe portraits are some of the best-known examples of pop art.

## The National Baseball Hall of Fame

All baseball players dream of being invited to Cooperstown, a small town in upstate New York. Why? Because Cooperstown is home to the National Baseball Hall of Fame, where baseball's greatest players are remembered. Since it opened in 1939, the Hall of Fame has selected only a few players each year. The Hall of Fame museum holds a massive collection of baseball items—from Yankee legend Babe Ruth's hat to modern Yankee David Wells's shoes. ■

New art styles continue to rise from Manhattan's artist communities. Artists live, work, and exhibit their art in neighborhoods such as Greenwich Village, SoHo, Chelsea, and TriBeCa.

## New York Sports

If any state can claim to be the birthplace of baseball, it is New York. According to legend, baseball was invented by Abner Doubleday in Cooperstown, New York, in 1839. But today, baseball historians agree that a New Yorker named Alexander Cartwright wrote the first set of official rules in 1845. These rules are very similar to today's version. The first game between two teams organized under Cartwright's rules occurred in Hoboken, New Jersey, on June 19, 1846. In four innings, the New York Club defeated the New York Knickerbockers 23 to 1.

In 1903, a Baltimore team moved to New York City and became the New York Highlanders. Ten years later, they changed their name again, this time to the New York Yankees. The Yankees played poor baseball for several years before making the greatest trade in the history of sports. In 1920, the Boston Red Sox were

## Yankee Stadium

In 1923, the Yankees moved into their new home in the Bronx—Yankee Stadium. Soon, the stadium echoed with the roar of fans and the thunderous crack of Babe Ruth's bat as he hammered his many home runs. Ruth's success launched the Yankees to stardom, and Yankee Stadium is called "the house that Ruth built."

Yankee Stadium is more than just a ballpark. When Pope Paul VI (in 1965) and Pope John Paul II (in 1979) came to New York City, they both stopped there to lead tens of thousands in a mass. When Nelson Mandela—the South African hero and leader—visited New York City in the early 1990s, Mayor David Dinkins brought him before a cheering crowd at Yankee Stadium. ■

**Babe Ruth**

struggling with high debt and offered their best player—Babe Ruth—to the New York Yankees.

When Ruth joined the Yankees, baseball was in a crisis. A year before, eight players on the Chicago White Sox purposely lost the World Series. The scandal shattered fan confidence in the game, and owners feared that attendance would plummet. The style of baseball was also different from today. The baseball was larger and heavier, and home runs were rare. This was known as the "dead ball" era of baseball.

In 1920, new rules prevented pitchers from throwing scruffed balls or spitball pitches. A new ball was introduced that seemed to jump off the bat. Suddenly, Babe Ruth started hitting home runs at an unbelievable rate—54 in 1920; 59 in 1921; 60 in 1927! No one had ever done this before. Soon, other players

A native New Yorker and Columbia University graduate, Henry Louis ("Lou") Gehrig (1903–1941), joined the New York Yankees in 1925. An outstanding hitter, Gehrig batted over .300 every season from 1926 to 1937. But Gehrig's accomplishments remained in the shadow of his flashy teammate, Babe Ruth. Gehrig's greatest accomplishment came from his ability to play every day. Known as the Iron Man, Gehrig played in 2,130 consecutive games—a record that remained unchallenged until Cal Ripken Jr. surpassed it in 1995.

## Lou Gehrig

In 1939, Gehrig discovered that he was suffering from amyotrophic lateral sclerosis (ALS, or now commonly called Lou Gehrig's disease—an incurable disease of the nervous system). He would never play again. Despite this realization, on July 4, 1939, Gehrig stood in front of the Yankee Stadium crowd and bravely proclaimed himself "the luckiest man on the face of the earth." He died two years later, a Yankee legend. ■

copied Ruth and set off a home-run explosion. Led by Ruth, the Yankees started to win World Series after World Series.

For the next fifty years, the Yankees dominated America's pastime. Whenever the Yankees appeared to be fading, a new star arrived and carried the team on his shoulders. Babe Ruth was succeeded by Lou Gehrig; Lou Gehrig yielded to Joe DiMaggio; Joe DiMaggio gave way to Mickey Mantle. But these players were more than just Yankees; they became national heroes, and their achievements were admired by fans everywhere. The Yankees became America's team and the most successful sports franchise in history, winning their twenty-fourth World Series in 1998.

Several New York baseball teams have left the city. In 1957, the Brooklyn Dodgers moved to Los Angeles. The move was a bitter loss to Brooklyn, and the painful absence is felt to this day. Another

New York baseball team—the New York Giants—moved to San Francisco in 1957. In 1962, the New York Mets started playing in Queens, New York. The Mets' uniform colors combine the orange of the New York Giants and the blue of the Brooklyn Dodgers.

What is the only New York football team that plays in New York? It's a trick question. Only the Buffalo Bills still play in New York State. The other New York football teams—the Giants and the Jets—played in New York City before moving to nearby New Jersey. Most New York City football fans now take trains and buses for the short ride to the New Jersey Meadowlands to watch the Giants and Jets play.

If you don't like watching baseball or football, there are plenty of other sports in New York. Three National Hockey League (NHL) teams—the Buffalo Sabres, the New York Rangers, and the New York Islanders—play in New York. The New York Rangers skate in New York City's Madison Square Garden. The National Basketball Association (NBA) New York Knicks and the WNBA New York Liberty also play at the Garden. Opponents have always commented on the loud and intense New York crowd. Basketball great Michael Jordan, who loves pressure and hostile crowds, has played some of his greatest games in Madison Square Garden. Major League Soccer has also placed the New York/New Jersey Metrostars in the nearby Meadowlands sports complex.

## Joe Namath

In 1965, Joe Namath signed with the New York Jets for $400,000—an enormous sum that created great expectations. But he proved to be worth it. After guaranteeing a Super Bowl victory over the powerful Baltimore Colts, Namath led the Jets to the championship, shocking everyone but himself. Namath also starred off the field in movies and on TV—earning him the nickname Broadway Joe. ■

## Mark Messier

Before Mark Messier arrived in New York, the New York Rangers hockey team had not won a Stanley Cup since 1940. During the 1994 playoffs, Messier scored two goals during a crucial game. The jubilant Rangers went on to win the Stanley Cup. ■

New York has several universities and colleges that compete for national recognition. In western New York, the Syracuse Orangemen contend every year in the NCAA basketball tournament. In 1997, they battled all the way to the finals before losing to Kentucky. The U.S. Military Academy at West Point meets its rival, Navy, on the football field for one of the most famous events in sports.

New York has hosted the Winter Olympic Games twice—in 1932 and 1980. Both games were held in Lake Placid, a small town nestled within the majestic Adirondack Mountains. The 1980 games witnessed one of the most spectacular and memorable moments in U.S. Olympic history—the U.S. defeat of the USSR hockey team, called the "Miracle on Ice." Lake Placid hopes to host the Winter Olympics again sometime in the future.

## Recreation

Many tourists head for New York with just one destination in mind: either the awesome grandeur of Niagara Falls or the culture and entertainment of Manhattan. But New Yorkers know their state has much more to offer.

Hikers, campers, and mountain climbers enjoy the sheer beauty of New York's wilderness areas. Both Adirondack Park and Catskill Forest Preserve protect vast expanses of forestland for recreation. In the winter, snowy mountains and hills are great for skiing, bobsledding, snowboarding, and tobogganing. Olympic ski jumps at Lake Placid, in the Adirondacks, are among the finest in the world. A carnival atmosphere reigns during winter festivals in Saranac Lake and Syracuse.

Canoeing on the
Hudson River

The Thousand Islands, the Finger Lakes, Lake George, and hundreds of other spots attract vacationers for boating, fishing, and parasailing. More adventurous types go rock climbing or take rafts or canoes down the Hudson River, gliding between craggy, wooded cliffs.

It's easy to see why millions of people from all over the world visit New York every year. No matter which of New York's two worlds they come to see, the timeless beauty of these places is sure to remain in their hearts.

# Timeline

## United States History

**1607** The first permanent British settlement is established in North America at Jamestown.

**1620** Pilgrims found Plymouth Colony, the second permanent British settlement.

**1776** America declares its independence from England.

**1783** Treaty of Paris officially ends the Revolutionary War in America.

**1787** U.S. Constitution is written.

**1803** Louisiana Purchase almost doubles the size of the United States.

**1812–15** U.S. and Britain fight the War of 1812.

**1861–65** The North and South fight each other in the American Civil War.

## New York State History

**1524** Giovanni da Verrazano sails into New York Harbor, becoming the first European to reach New York.

**1609** Englishman Henry Hudson reaches the mouth of the Hudson River.

**1625** Dutch settlers begin building New Amsterdam (the future New York City).

**1664** The Dutch surrender New Amsterdam to England.

**1776** New York approves the Declaration of Independence.

**1788** New York becomes the eleventh state.

**1825** The Erie Canal opens.

**1831** New York's first railroad, the Mohawk and Hudson, begins running between Albany and Schenectady.

**1883** The Brooklyn Bridge opens, linking Manhattan with Brooklyn.

**1901** President William McKinley is assassinated in Buffalo.

# United States History

The United States is **1917–18** involved in World War I.

The stock market crashes, plunging **1929** the United States into the Great Depression.

The United States fights in **1941–45** World War II.

The United States becomes a **1945** charter member of the United Nations.

The United States fights **1951–53** in the Korean War.

The U.S. Congress enacts a series of **1964** groundbreaking civil rights laws.

The United States **1964–73** engages in the Vietnam War.

The United States and other **1991** nations fight the brief Persian Gulf War against Iraq.

# New York State History

**1911** Triangle Shirtwaist factory fire kills 146 women workers and leads to labor reforms.

**1939–40** New York City hosts a world's fair.

**1948** The first state university in New York is established.

**1952** The United Nations Headquarters is completed in New York City.

**1959** The St. Lawrence Seaway opens, allowing oceangoing vessels to use New York State ports on Lake Ontario and Lake Erie.

**1960** The New York State Thruway is completed.

**1964–65** Another world's fair is held in New York City.

**1967** The state legislature establishes a lottery.

**1971** A rebellion at the Attica State Correctional Facility ends with forty-three deaths.

# Fast Facts

New York

Bluebird

| | |
|---|---|
| **Statehood date** | July 26, 1788, the 11th state |
| **Origin of state name** | Named for the Duke of York |
| **State capital** | Albany |
| **State nickname** | Empire State |
| **State motto** | "*Excelsior*" (Ever upward) |
| **State bird** | Bluebird |
| **State flower** | Rose |
| **State fish** | Native brook trout |
| **State song** | "I Love New York" |
| **State tree** | Sugar maple |
| **State fruit** | Apple |
| **State animal** | Beaver |
| **State gem** | Wine-red garnet |
| **State fossil** | *Eurypterus remipes* |
| **State muffin** | Apple muffin |
| **State fair** | Syracuse (late August–early September) |
| **Total area; rank** | 53,989 sq. mi. (139,831 sq km); 27th |
| **Land; rank** | 47,224 sq. mi. (122,310 sq km); 30th |
| **Water; rank** | 6,765 sq. mi. (17,521 sq km); 5th |
| ***Inland water;* rank** | 1,888 sq. mi. (4,890 sq km); 10th |
| ***Coastal water;* rank** | 976 sq. mi. (2,528 sq km); 8th |
| ***Great Lakes water;* rank** | 3,901 sq. mi. (10,104 sq km); 3rd |

The Hudson River

Chinatown

| | |
|---|---|
| **Geographic center** | Madison, 12 miles (19 km) south of Oneida and 26 miles (42 km) southwest of Utica |
| **Latitude and longitude** | New York is located approximately between 40° 30' and 45° 00' N and 72° 10' and 79° 45' W |
| **Highest point** | Mount Marcy, 5,344 feet (1,629 m) |
| **Lowest point** | Sea level at the Atlantic Ocean |
| **Largest city** | New York City |
| **Number of counties** | 62 |
| **Population; rank** | 18,044,505 (1990 census); 2nd |
| **Density** | 367 persons per sq. mi. (142 per sq km) |
| **Population distribution** | 84% urban, 16% rural |

| **Ethnic distribution** | White | 74.40% |
|---|---|---|
| **(does not equal 100%)** | African-American | 15.89% |
| | Native American | 0.35% |
| | Hispanic | 12.31% |
| | Asian and Pacific Islande | 3.86% |
| | Other | 5.50% |

| | |
|---|---|
| **Record high temperature** | 108°F (42°C) at Troy on July 22, 1926 |
| **Record low temperature** | −52°F (−47°C) at Old Forge, on February 18, 1979 |
| **Average July temperature** | 69°F (21°C) |
| **Average January temperature** | 21°F (−6°C) |
| **Average annual precipitation** | 39 inches (99 cm) |

# Natural Areas and Historic Sites

### National Historic Sites

**The Women's Rights National Historical Park**

*Eleanor Roosevelt National Historic Site* (Hyde Park) was the First Lady's home, Val-Kill.

*Home of Franklin D. Roosevelt National Historic Site* is the U.S. president's birthplace and lifelong home.

*Martin Van Buren National Historic Site* is the retirement home of the U.S. president.

*Sagamore Hill National Historic Site* is the home of Theodore Roosevelt from 1886 to 1919.

*Saint Paul's Church National Historic Site* preserves a church important to the American Revolution.

*Theodore Roosevelt Birthplace National Historic Site* preserves the U.S. president's birthplace in New York City.

*Theodore Roosevelt Inaugural National Historic Site* preserves the Ansley Wilcox House in Buffalo, where the vice president took the oath of office upon the assassination of President William McKinley.

*Vanderbilt Mansion National Historic Site* is a stately mansion along the Hudson River.

### National Historical Parks

*Saratoga National Historical Park* is the site of an important American Revolution battle.

*Women's Rights National Historical Park* memorializes the place of the important early meetings for equal rights for women in the United States.

### National Monuments

*Castle Clinton National Monument* is a structure in lower New York City that once defended New York Harbor.

*Fort Stanwix National Monument* commemorates the site of important American Revolutionary defense against the British.

**Snowy Mountain**

*Statue of Liberty National Monument* is home to the massive statue that has become a worldwide symbol of freedom.

### National Scenic and Recreation River

*Upper Delaware National Scenic and Recreation River* is 73 miles (118 km) of free-flowing river along the New York and Pennsylvania border.

### State Parks

New York has nearly 200 state parks and forest preserves. *Adirondack Park* is the largest state park in the United States, at 6 million acres (2.4 million ha).

## Sports Teams

### NCAA Teams (Division I)

Canisius College Golden Griffins

Colgate University Red Raiders

Columbia University Lions

Cornell University Big Red

Fordham University Rams

Hofstra University Flying Dutchmen

Iona College Gaels

Long Island University Blackbirds

Manhattan College Jaspers

Marist College Red Foxes

Niagara University Purple Eagles

Siena College Saints

St. Bonaventure University Bonnies

St. Francis College Terriers

St. John's University Red Storm

State University of New York–Buffalo Bulls

Syracuse University Orangemen

U.S. Military Academy Black Knights

Wagner College Seahawks

**Major League Baseball**

New York Mets

New York Yankees

**National Basketball Association**

New York Knickerbockers

**National Football Association**

Buffalo Bills

New York Jets

New York Giants

**National Hockey League**

New York Rangers

Buffalo Sabres

New York Islanders

**Women's National Basketball Association**

New York Liberty

**The Baseball Hall of Fame**

## Cultural Institutions

### Libraries

*The New York Public Library* is the largest public library in the nation.

*Columbia University Library* (New York City) and *Cornell University Library* (Ithaca) are among the largest collections in the world.

*Pierpont Morgan Library* (New York City) is a large special library with fine examples of early printing and manuscripts.

**The Metropolitan Musuem of Art**

*Franklin D. Roosevelt Library* (Hyde Park) is the official library for the thirty-second president of the United States.

**Museums**

New York City is home to a large number of the finest museums in the world: *the Solomon R. Guggenheim Museum, the Metropolitan Museum of Art, the Museum of Modern Art,* and *the Whitney Museum of American Art.*

*The National Baseball Hall of Fame and Museum* (Cooperstown)

*The Museum of Glass* (Corning)

*The State Museum* (Albany)

**Performing Arts**

New York has sixteen major opera companies, eleven major symphony orchestras, thirty-five major dance companies, and six major nonprofit theater companies.

**Universities and Colleges**

In the mid-1990s, New York had 88 public and 226 private institutions of higher learning.

## Annual Events

**January–March**

Bobsled and luge competitions in Lake Placid (every weekend, January through mid-March)

Ski jumping competitions in Lake Placid (early January and mid-March)

Winterfest in Syracuse (mid-February)

Westminster Kennel Club Dog Show in New York City (February)

Winter Carnival in Saranac Lake (February)

St. Patrick's Day Parade in New York City (March)

## April–June

Schoharie County Maple Festival in Jefferson (May)

Hudson River White Water Derby in North Creek (May)

National Lake Trout Derby on Seneca Lake near Geneva (May)

Festival of Lilacs in Rochester (May)

Empire State Regatta in Albany (June)

A Festival of Gold in the Niagara region (mid-April–mid-May)

Belmont Stakes Horse Race on Long Island (early June)

## July–September

Jazz Festival New York in New York City, Saratoga Springs, and Canandaigua (July)

Annual Summer Ski Jump in Lake Placid (July)

German Alps Festival in Hunter, near Tannersville (July)

Friendship Festival in Buffalo (July)

Mormon Religious Pageant at Hill Cumorah near Palmyra (mid-July)

National Baseball Hall of Fame Induction Ceremony in Cooperstown (late July or early August)

Central New York Scottish Games in Liverpool (August)

United States Tennis Association Championships in Flushing Meadow, Queens (late August and early September)

Pulaski Salmon Festival (September)

Adirondack Hot Air Balloon Festival in Glens Falls (September)

## October–December

Oyster Festival in Oyster Bay, Long Island (October)

Thanksgiving Day Parade in New York City (November)

Annual Snowbird Soaring Regatta at Elmira (late November)

**The Saratoga Race Track**

**Lake Placid village**

Festival of Lights in Niagara Falls (Thanksgiving to early January)

Rockefeller Center Tree Lighting Ceremony in New York City (December)

**Theodore Roosevelt**

**Franklin D. Roosevelt**

## Famous People

| | |
|---|---|
| Humphrey Bogart (1899–1957) | Actor |
| James Cagney (1899–1986) | Actor |
| Millard Fillmore (1800–1874) | U.S. president |
| Henry Louis (Lou) Gehrig (1903–1941) | Baseball player |
| George Gershwin (1898–1937) | Composer |
| Jackie Gleason (1916–1987) | Entertainer |
| Julia Ward Howe (1819–1910) | Social reformer |
| Washington Irving (1783–1859) | Author |
| Henry James (1843–1916) | Author |
| Herman Melville (1819–1891) | Author |
| George Mortimer Pullman (1831–1897) | Inventor and industrialist |
| John D. Rockefeller (1839–1937) | Industrialist and philanthropist |
| Eleanor Roosevelt (1884–1962) | U.S. First Lady |
| Franklin D. Roosevelt (1882–1945) | U.S. president |
| Theodore Roosevelt (1858–1919) | U.S. president |
| Elizabeth Cady Stanton (1815–1902) | Suffragist |
| Martin Van Buren (1782–1862) | U.S. president |
| Walt Whitman (1819–1892) | Poet |

# To Find Out More

## History

- Chambers, Veronica. *The Harlem Renaissance*. Broomall, Penn.: Chelsea House, 1997.

- Doherty, Craig A. *The Empire State Building*. Woodbridge, Conn.: Blackbirch, 1998.

- Mann, Elizabeth, and Alan Witschonke (illus.). *The Brooklyn Bridge: A Wonders of the World Book*. New York: Mikaya Press, 1996.

- Fradin, Dennis Brindell. *New York*. Chicago: Childrens Press, 1993.

- Fradin, Dennis Brindell. *The New York Colony*. Chicago: Childrens Press, 1988.

- Tagliaferro, Linda. *Destination New York*. Minneapolis: Lerner, 1998.

- Kallen, Stuart A., and Kristen Copham (illus.). *Statue of Liberty Poem*. Edina, Minn.: Abdo & Daughters, 1994.

- Kent, Deborah. *New York City*. Danbury, Conn.: Children's Press, 1996.

- Miller, Natalie. *The Statue of Liberty*. Chicago: Childrens Press, 1992.

## Fiction

- Konigsburg, E. L. *From the Mixed-Up Files of Mrs. Basil E. Frankweiler*. New York: Atheneum, 1970.

- Seldon, George, and Garth Williams (illus.). *The Cricket in Times Square*. South Holland, Ill.: Yearling Books, 1970.

- Taylor, Sydney. *All-Of-A-Kind Family*. South Holland, Ill.: Yearling Books, 1980.

## Biography

- Osinski, Alice. *Franklin D. Roosevelt: Thirty-second President of the United States*. Chicago: Childrens Press, 1988.

## Websites

- **New York State Website**
  *http://www.state.ny.us/*
  New York State's official website

- **I Love New York**
  *http://www.iloveny.state.ny.us/*
  New York's complete guide to travel and tourism in the Empire State

## Addresses

- **New York State Division of Tourism**
  1 Commerce Plaza
  Albany, NY 12245
  For information about travel and tourism

- **Department of State**
  162 Washington Avenue
  Albany, NY 12231
  For information about New York's government

- **New York State Museum**
  Room 3099
  Cultural Education Center
  Albany, NY 12230
  For information about New York's history

# Index

Page numbers in *italics* indicate illustrations.

# Meet the Author

Ann Heinrichs fell in love with faraway places while reading Doctor Dolittle books as a child. She has traveled through most of the United States and several countries in Europe, as well as northwest Africa, the Middle East, and east Asia. Both business and pleasure have taken her to New York many times.

"Trips are fun, but the real work—tracking down all the factual information for a book—begins at the library. I head straight for the reference department. Some of my favorite resources are statistical abstracts and the library's computer databases.

"For this book, I also read local newspapers from several cities in New York. The Internet was a super research tool, too. The Library of Congress website offers first-person accounts by New Yorkers in the 1920s. And the state library and various state agencies have websites that are chock full of information.

"To me, writing nonfiction is a bigger challenge than writing fiction. With nonfiction, you can't just dream something up—everything has to be researched. When I uncover the facts, they always turn out to be more spectacular than fiction could ever be."

Ann Heinrichs grew up in Arkansas and lives in Chicago. She is the author of more than thirty books for children and young adults on American, Asian, and African history and culture. (*Tibet* and *Egypt,* in Children's Press's Enchantment of the World series, were awarded honorable mention by the National Federation of Press Women.)

Ms. Heinrichs has also written numerous newspaper, magazine, and encyclopedia articles and critical reviews. As an advertising copywriter, she has covered everything from plumbing hardware to Oriental rugs. She holds a bachelor's and master's degree in piano performance. These days, her performing arts are t'ai chi chuan and kung fu sword.

# Photo Credits